ALSO BY J.D. SCRIMGEOUR

POETRY

Small, Rectangular, Reflected World
香蕉面包 *Banana Bread*
Festival
Lifting the Turtle
Territories
The Last Miles

NONFICTION

Waiting in the 21st Century (with Maryellen Groot, Yufei Hu, and Devyn Verruto)
Themes for English B: A Professor's Education In and Out of Class
Spin Moves

CD

Ogunquit & Other Works (with Philip Swanson)

EDITOR

As Only True Can Be: James R. Scrimgeour Selected Poems
9x5

POET IN HIGH STREET PARK

PROSE & POETRY FOR MODERN SALEM

POET IN HIGH STREET PARK

PROSE & POETRY FOR MODERN SALEM

J.D. SCRIMGEOUR

LP

Loom Press
Amesbury, Massachusetts
2026

ISBN: 978-0-931507-56-4

Printed in the United States of America
First edition

Design: Keith Finch
Author photograph: Eileen FitzGerald
Font: Rig Shaded, Caslon Pro
Printing: Versa Press, Illinois

Loom Press
15 Atlantic View, Amesbury, Massachusetts 01913
www.loompress.com
info@loompress.com

Acknowledgments are listed in the back of the book.

for Aidan and Guthrie

CONTENTS

Introduction: *This is Megan's Swing*

"I found you a job," Eileen said. She was looking through *The Chronicle of Higher Education*. "Salem State College. Assistant Professor of Creative Writing, Poetry."

It was the winter of 1996. We were in Greencastle, Indiana, sharing a temporary teaching position. We had a nine-month-old son, whom we would swap as one of us left the house to teach after the other had finished. I had torn my ACL a month earlier, and I was scheduled for surgery in April.

The job seemed promising. It was on the East Coast, where my family lived. Both my parents had been born in Massachusetts. Although I had never been to Salem, I had heard about it for the previous decade. My father had done genealogy research there and discovered that an ancestor in our direct line, Mary Towne Eastey, had been put to death during the witchcraft hysteria of the 1600s. Another ancestor, Thomas Perkins, sat on the jury that found her guilty.

I sent off my application—one of over 500 I sent out over three years—and was invited to do a phone interview. During it, I mentioned my family's history. "We don't do that anymore," one of the committee members assured me.

Soon after, I was invited to a campus interview, but Salem State was so strapped for cash they wouldn't pay for all my travel expenses. Eileen and I were burdened by student loans and a new baby, and we weighed whether it was worth it to make the trip. My uncle came to my rescue, offering his frequent flyer miles, and so I found myself in a small conference room in Meier Hall, talking about how Yusef Komunyakaa and Sharon Olds use metaphor.

After the interview, my parents, who were on a brief vacation in nearby Gloucester, picked me up and drove me to their motel on the beach. It was night by then, and I called Eileen on the room's phone to share how things had gone. I stretched the cord and held the receiver to the sliding screen door to the porch. "Do you hear that?" I asked. "It's the ocean."

Although the ocean was probably less than 100 yards away, as I stood there peering out through the screen, it wasn't visible. A thick fog made it impossible to see more than a few yards in front of me. The surf, like the future, was out there—loud, constant—but I'd need to wait to see it.

On the return from Indianapolis, where I'd had my knee surgery, I was pretty doped up. Eileen drove me back, with Aidan, in a car seat on the passenger side facing backwards, gazing at me as I lay across the back seat, nauseous, trying to slip into sleep. Every so often, I would lean over and puke in a bucket on the floor, and Aidan would laugh. That's not how mouths are supposed to work!

Eileen helped me inside and onto our sofa, and a minute later came back into the room to tell me that Salem State's dean had left a message on the answering machine, asking to return her call. I couldn't wait. Eileen pulled the phone over to me, and I called. When the dean offered me the job, I said, "I think I want to accept, but I'm just out of surgery and on a lot of pain medications. I was instructed not to make any important life decisions in the next 24 hours."

The next day, I accepted the offer. And, you could say, I discovered my life.

While I wasn't born in Salem, I've lived here 30 years. The city has become the water I swim in, something I don't always notice because it just is, it's just a part of me.

And I literally swim in Salem. This past week as summer eases in, Eileen and I have driven out to Waikiki beach on Winter Island and jumped into the ocean at that sheltered cove. Once the water was deliciously cold, another time achingly so. That second time I only managed to dive in before scrambling out to go read in my beach chair.

Winter Island is not an island, though it was when the colonists named it. Waikiki Beach was named much later, in the mid-20th century, when the

Coast Guard had an air station, and some service members who had been stationed in Hawaii gave the name to the quiet stretch of sand. How things get named. I like the quirkiness of Waikiki, but it's probably not a name the city residents would have chosen. And Winter Island? Over time, that name has become just wrong.

This book contains three decades of my own idiosyncratic naming.

I've walked or biked down many of Salem's streets, and I've attended my share of community activities. I've experienced the glorious Haunted Happenings parade the first Thursday evening of October, in which half the city marches and performs for the other half, as well as for the tourists who clog the city's streets each fall, like fat in the arteries. I've sat on committees and made public comments at city government meetings. Still, my Salem has revolved around a few spots. One is High Street Park, a humble park on a small side street just two blocks from my house where I have brought my sons since their infancy, and which I still visit occasionally to shoot baskets. The teens who hang out there now know me and give me my space, and if the courts are taken when I arrive, I turn back and give them theirs. The park has come to stand in my mind for the neighborhood, and for the Salem community in general, for the idea of community.

Another location is the classrooms of Salem State, where I have spent much of my energy these past 30 years, listening to students, helping them find the words they need to tell their stories.

Salem State College, the place I began my career, is no more. It's now Salem State University, a renaming that happened in 2010. It is hard to say if it has made any difference. The student body has changed somewhat, becoming darker-skinned and a little poorer, but the school itself has held to its mission. It remains an affordable option for those with little money, and a second chance for those whose first college experience didn't take.

Over the course of my tenure, I have moved offices eight times. My second office was on the third floor of the old Salem State Library, which was condemned, at a moment's notice, in 2007. I remember receiving an email at 10 in the morning, saying that I needed to vacate the premises by noon. We could only return to clean out our offices via police escort, wearing a hard hat.

Apparently, when the building was built in the 1970s, they hadn't taken into account the weight of the books, and the cantilevered spaces, including my office, were in danger of falling off the sides. When I helped students clear out the office of Salem State's national literary magazine, *Soundings East*, also in one of these spaces, we moved a filing cabinet and discovered a crack that widened to nearly half a foot where the office was (supposedly) attached to the rest of the building. Needless to say, I made it out alive.

A third touchstone is Forest River Park. It's just two blocks from Salem State, but the world there is separate, local: from the community pool, recently renovated, to the absurd cement slide (yes, a cement slide), to the Little League fields, where I spent a good decade of my life, coaching my sons. There are moments when I wish I had some of those hours on the ballfield back—to travel the world, to see more art and music in Boston, to read and write—but that time made me know Salem in ways I could not have otherwise. It's where I experienced the intersection of the city's population, a place where Salem's white working class and the growing Dominican community could not avoid each other. The parents sat next to each other on the bleachers. The children were teammates.

A few years after I had finished coaching, one short story came to me, then a whole flood of them. I hadn't written much fiction, but the genre, and the sport, seemed perfect to explore the social dynamics I witnessed at the park. Some of those stories are represented here.

There are more places, of course. Even as I write, the Peabody Essex Museum prods: *What about me*? Yes, before your millions of dollars of renovations, I pushed a stroller through dusty dark rooms past your whale skeleton, your aisles of taxidermized birds. There's the Salem Athenaeum, where I've served as chair of the Writing Committee and led the Salem Writers Group for over two decades. It has a claim, the place in the world where I've heard the most good language. And then there are the Ropes Garden, Harbor Sweets, Red's Restaurant, the Gulu-Gulu café, the insipid *Bewitched* statue . . . . The list keeps growing: Salem High School, The Salem Y, The Willows . . . . They are all raising their hands, asking to be called on.

But these three places—the neighborhood, the school, the diamond—are what gives this book its structure and grounding as it explores themes of community, class, and race in this city. They are what I know.

Mary Eastey was tried twice and found guilty of witchcraft both times, though after a month in jail following the first conviction her case was reviewed, and she was briefly set free. At that first trial, Nathaniel Hawthorne's ancestor, Judge Hathorne, presided.

After she was sentenced to death the second time, Mary Eastey, in a letter to the governor, asked that "no more innocent blood be shed."

"I petition to your honors not for my own life, for I know I must die, and my appointed time is set . . . I know not the least thing of witchcraft, therefore I cannot, I durst not, belie my own soul." She was hanged the next day.

Three hundred and thirty-three years later, Salem selected a descendant of Mary Eastey to be the city's first poet laureate. Sometimes I think about that.

Salem's rich, complex history is daunting to a writer. There's simply too much. And many words have already been spilled on it. This book looks at the Great Salem Fire of 1914 and peeks in on the Peabody sisters, but its focus is modern Salem, everyday life in this old city.

Especially in these bleak times for our country, I wish my writing could bring an end to some injustice, the way Mary Eastey's petition helped bring an end to the witch trials. These words, though, will need to content themselves with simply being part of the historical record, a testimony that beneath the Halloween hoo-ha and the historical tours crowding the sidewalks, people lived here.

And these people, like me, claimed this place as their own, whether it's Tony, the janitor taking classes at Salem State, hoping to become a high-school teacher, or Miguel, the Dominican teen in "Prospect," who relinquishes his dreams of a baseball career and finds that Salem offers new dreams, or Megan, the girl I'll never know, who left the note on a swing at High Street Park that I was fortunate enough to find: *This is Megan's swing*.

—JDS, 2025

Salem, Mass

I hope I never forget that pack of middle-schoolers
at the playground near my house, how they acted
like middle-schoolers, shouting their conversations
across the neighborhood as if showing off new sneakers,
the boys doing mean things to the girls,
the girls saying mean things about each other.
If I hadn't been at the jungle gym with my two-year-old,
I'm sure they would have been smashing bottles
on the basketball court.

Then, like pigeons when popcorn spills,
they flocked to a spot under the basket.
Some squealed. A boy held out his arm,
keeping others back. "It's alive," I heard one say,
and suddenly one boy was cupping a baby bird
in his hand as another climbed the pole
that held up the net. "Give it to me,"
said the boy on the pole, and he took the bird
and placed it in the nest that was behind the backboard.

Too much misery goes down
in this city I call my home. I'm in no mood
to list it here, now. In my children's schools,
the schools where my wife teaches,
it's all too clear which kids won't get past
their dead mother, their addicted father, the fact
that no one has ever read them a book . . . .

It was just one small bird
who must have had a stupid parent—
who would build a nest
on the backside of a backboard?—
but that afternoon it was safe,
and as I chased my son, trying to stop him
from stepping in the dog shit,
the voices of the middle-schoolers fading
as they made their way up the block
to go play video games and pretend to kill things,
as I held his hand while he zipped down the slide
I thought, yeah, I guess I could live here
for the rest of my life.

THE NEIGHBORHOOD

Prayer

Don't you know that love is holy
can't you see that I am only
all the things you've told to me

and when I ask to be forgiven
for the ways I've failed at living
will you sing a song to me

Montage of Brick and Water

Beating the Bounds (the City Limits)

Hawthorne hated it—the assumptions
of power, the majesty of money,
crushing as brick. Horses, and streets
that narrow near the water, spray
of sea across a face, an ungloved hand,
stones beating each other into smoothness
in the surf, beating the bounds, rounding
brick to pebble, to sand. 1692 . . .

1962. The generals disappearing from their
families for ten days, debating Cuba.
This country that started here, nearly
extinguished. Now, should the masks
get handed out, they'll be gone before
Salem gets any.

Hopeful? What's the difference between
5 years and 80? The death of a child,
an old woman? Between millions
and thousands? Between boulders
and pebbles? Sand through the fingers
trickling on a warm, sunscreened leg.
Sand emptied from sneakers
onto the brick porch. Drinking
filtered water, piano blinking
runs of notes. Spill of waves.

Brick

More are cracked than whole,
none quite the same color
though they can be painted,
usually white or black.

They make painful, brief music
chipping, cutting the hand—

they gather in wheelbarrows . . .
and, mortared into the Essex Condos,
they rise out of the downtown,
casting their shadows
over the pedestrian mall.

The Shoreline

On the shoreline swollen gulls stand guard,
while others sit back a few feet,
bellies on the sand—a coffee break.

Several twist and tuck their heads
into the feathers along their side
as if nursing themselves,
or reaching for their wallets.

Their legs are their proudest parts.
Spindly, they concentrate
strength and orange.

Those pairs of mallards frisking in the surf
are too content, and too simple
for these gulls, who will

squabble and cry over french fries,
who will fly off, alone, if the wind
moves them, catches them right.

Cigar Store Indian, Salem, Massachusetts, April 1999

Split from shoulder to gut,
he grins. Only half a man,
he's got no backside, guarding
the five-and-dime's trinkets
behind him, behind glass: a ceramic
Groucho, who looks mulatto,
and a Mark Twain. His grin–
so stupid—at first arouses pity,
but look closer: it's unbelievable.
          Across Washington Street
insidc a monolith of brick, someone
named Aracely sells witch-hangings
in an anonymous office. Residents
get loans to delead their houses
before their children become
idiots.

If he could see,
he'd see down the alley
the building where Bell first
displayed the phone. If he could
remember, he'd remember the murmur
of the river in the distance,
now dry and paved; the warm stink
of horse dung on the cobblestones.
He'd remember those pimple nights
when, kidnapped for thrills,
he lurched in the back of pick-ups.
He was always found—in the woods
a few yards off Route 1A,
or face down on Gallows Hill.
Unlike the Pope, he won't make
the millennium. Gash deepening
and widening, he'll be gone
before this poem is finished,
replaced and used for fuel.

Way Back

It used to be.
It used to be.

They've dedicated the Little League field
beside Pioneer Village—where men
and women dressed in 17th century clothes
furtively chase two rats that—they say—
someone set free there.

The name: Stephen O'Grady,
beloved coach, killed
by a drunk driver
outside the bounds.

That Guy You See Around Sometimes

Baggy pants, black hair shagged,
unshaven, 22, he holds

his three-year-old's hand into
High Street Park—the one

with no grass behind
what used to be

the St. Mary's Italian
Catholic Church. The boy

lets go for the steps
to the slide as he tells

an older father—the only
other adult there—how

he works at the Hawthorne
Hotel, he'd like to go to college

someday, how the mother
walked out eight months ago—

"wants nothing to do with him,"
chin pointing toward the boy,

voice without bitterness,
just heavy with astonishment

at the world's thoughtlessness—
"Joshua," he calls, "Joshua,"

and moves to catch his son.

Apologies

It is not my story, the story
of my ancestors, Mary T. Eastey,
hung for witchcraft, Thomas
Perkins, one of the jurors
who found her guilty, it
is not my story, not yet.

No, I write of basements flooded
and duct-taped cars, private schools
in surrounding towns shimmering
with playing fields, their
nutrient-enriched grass like a shag rug,
and public school children that ride
buses to dark, borrowed gyms,
recess on a small asphalt playground
with some painted bases
alongside the college students, passing
class to class, cigarettes and—

Hawthorne hated it all, hated it—
wrote romances in which the good,
the simple good, triumphed. The rule
of order flawed from the start.

Salem in Myth and Memory

The power plant manager
arguing against the new regulations

at the meeting with the state reps
in the College's 800-seat

auditorium overflowing with
community, saying, "This

is an injustice as bad
as the witch hunts!"
                    Some

in the crowd hissing, those
in white helmets applauding.

Overheard

Who said
the food
at Red's
is good?

Roll Call

St. Mary's Italian Catholic Church,
closed in 2003, after 85 years—brick.

Salem State College Library—brick.

The boxy mansions of Chestnut Street
("the most beautiful street in America")—brick.
The facade of the old armory before
they demolished it—brick.

The sidewalks that ruin strollers—brick.

Our house, built after the great fire of 1914—
we've been told that between the drywall inside
and the asbestos shingles outside,
a layer of brick.

Buck-A-Bag

I used to play basketball Saturday mornings,
spend the afternoon reading on a shaded porch.
Now people coo at my back, talk monosyllables
to Guthrie, my nine-month-old in this Unitarian
Universalist church that ministers to gays,
lesbians, and public defenders, and which is now
selling old clothes on folding tables and claiming
to sell donuts, though I don't see any, and even
if I did, that's not what we're here for, not with 100
chocolate-and-butterscotch-chip cookies at home
for the Fischer-Urkowitzes this evening, as if
they will eat even 10 of them—who are we kidding?—
we make the cookies to eat them ourselves, we make
sure that we'll have enough and so no donuts, no
basketball—no, this is get other people's
trash almost free! Typewriters needing ribbons.

Updike paperbacks. 1000-piece puzzles of Amsterdam
at night with mini-lights that you insert—batteries
not included. A 20, no 10, no 5-dollar bike.

My older son, Aidan, has opened one of the games,
"Where in the World," and is rapidly memorizing
all the countries in Asia, circa 1986. Eileen,
my wife, is being handed not just clothes, but
their histories, from a woman who is emptying
her garbage bag of donations. She just gave
Eileen a pair of shorts that would barely fit
over my wrists. Oh, where is the man
in the gray sweatshirt who wants to give
everything away? I'd pay a quarter for that puzzle,
but not 50 cents, no way.

Barbara and Bella

Two sisters, one
who never talks, one
who never stops, how

there used to be a market
where CVS is and we'd get
buttah, sure, and meat—

the phone call during the storm:
you tell him he can't shovel snow
in front of your house
look outside, go look outside.

They both call Eileen Ellen.
Bella says, *oh Barbara,*
tell them about the owl.

Oh yeah, we saw an owl
right there on our porch,
real tiny, right up—

her hand, blotchy and curled
stiff from the years
at Sylvania, rises and moves
as if tossing seed—*there.*

Failed Poetry Exercise

If at first you don't succeed
you're doing it wrong. Like teaching:

I give them gum, and a first line.
They offer both back, the gum

already chewed, of course, sweetness
and firmness dispersed in their

arid mouths. And I do care if they
write poems, the way I care

that the cop who died in the crash
had young twins. Kim, straight

from the funeral and its traffic,
didn't want to talk about Hawthorne

seizing the public by the button,
but she did since I'd written it

in my datebook: *March 31. Kim,*
4:00: Hawthorne, button.

Before leaving we both almost wept.

To Be Ignored

The Board of Education
orders us to "Buckle Down."

Jury Duty

No room
in the county courthouse,
so they're shuttled across
Federal Street.

The hour rolls by
in the church basement—
the video over
that explains the duties.

Signs abound:

We are all God's children

Proclaim Liberty

Hope

Peace

Love

Joy

Taped to a pole: *Please put all trash in barrels.*

So many talking . . .
one man explains solitaire to a woman.

Pigeon #3

On the roof of the Senior Center
sit a line of pigeons

turning their heads
from street to graveyard.

They coo and caw,
sharing info: spilled fries
on Endicott,
cat's out on Winthrop.

That one with the swath
of white on its side, third
from the left, longs to poke
among the cigarette butts

surrounding the trash can,
if only to get away
from the gabbing. Instead,
it ruffles its feathers and

pecks at a noisy neighbor,
then flicks its head
into the gutter and grinds
pebbles in its beak.

Salem to Lynn: A Note

Lynn, you've lost your shoes.
Maybe someone stole them
down Long Beach. Watch

your step, girl, there's glass
and hypodermic needles
in the sand.

July 4

I didn't know about the Horribles Parade
at Salem Willows, and I didn't know

whether the buses were running when the lone
man asked.

Of course, the flags were hacking the sky,
but after a while they stopped and hung,
spent . . .

The scent of lighter fluid in the air . . .

In the slice of park, under a huddle of trees,
a few sit on benches, pigeons walking

at their feet.

The Labontes have a large, sturdy sign
in their front yard. Their name, cursive,
above a painting of Joseph, Mary, and baby Jesus.

And the parking lot sign with "Private" whited out:
Property.

Salem Willows

What is the meaning of life? Which popcorn—
wintergreen, molasses, or buttered—
is the best? Miniature golf squeezed
between the tired arcades, teens
driving and skiing and killing
wildly, dying over and over.

For a dime, the aged monkeys
dance in their glass cage, their necks
worn through, fur half gone,
clothes untucked. For a nickel
the drinking test: worming a metal circle
around a curved, electrified bar. Are you
Punch Drunk? Pickled?

The Sights

After illicit ejaculation
in a Chestnut Street bedroom,
the bodies pause, then rise
and prepare for the other side
of the shades where the trolley
shimmies and announces facts
like bricks, canned jokes the mortar.

At dusk,
groups of tourists clutching candles
trudge through the empty downtown
realizing they could be somewhere
else. The guide, draped in cliché black,
can't muster a reason . . .

The bricks, though, clutch the past,
hoping to contain it in sidewalks and walls.
Fragments wash up on Dead Horse Beach
and Forest River, not quite smooth,
and plainly different—more fragile,
less beautiful, than rock.

Atlantic Blues

Heard the weather last night
hurting the shore.
Heard the surf last night
just *hurting* the shore.
Don't know why I left.
Won't do it no more.

Saw the water this morning,
a sheet of blue.
Saw the water this morning,
a long sheet of blue.
It's a go-home day.
That's what I'm gonna do.

Felt the water today
rise up past my knees.
Felt the cold Atlantic
and an arctic breeze.
It's a hard luck world.
Take me back, please!

North Street Shell

Have you prayed to Allah today?
read the small sign
over the penny dish

that disappeared from the gas station
after nine-eleven. And when

that October, a customer
asks the Arabic counterman
"Things going o.k. for you?

Any problems?" He shrugs,
says, "It's o.k.," says,
"What're you gonna do?"

Walking Winthrop Street

The ice-pocked sidewalk leads me
to walk in the street, and the world
takes on an astonishing balance:

houses the same distance from me,
sidewalks like rails,
And the telephone poles and light poles

rise sheer into the night, the pools
of light in clear patterns. Only
the trees don't line up, spilling their shadows

wherever they fall, hovering
over the wires and bulbs.

The Family

Lynn smokes a pack a day. She married Peabody when she got pregnant. Now they hardly talk. Her children have stolen from her, sold her VCR for drug money. She sits on the stoop each morning, smoking, her bleached hair drying in the sun.

Peabody works in the aged coffee shop. A stained apron. Balding. His brother works with him, and they each plot who will take over the business once the grandmother, who speaks no English, dies.

Salem is the grandmother, tottering, senile. She calls for her sister, long dead, when she wakes in the night. Her hands gnarl the cross round her neck. Teenagers furtively bring her babies to strangle in the shadows of dawn. No one knows what happens then. No one has ever told.

Beverly is ashamed of his brother, but also of himself. Growing up, he was teased for having a girl's name. He's hated working in the shop, him with a college degree. He won't speak Greek, claims he has forgotten, but he listens closely to grandmother's mutterings at the Thanksgiving table.

Yellow Leaves on a Blue Plastic Slide

Which gleams more brightly,
death or childhood?
Or is it their juxtaposition
that gives each its shine?

Just beyond this playground
runs the train, then the river.
One empties into the city,
the other, the sea.

The Masthead

You could have a hundred
gables, your house on the sea
would still be smaller than leaves
of grass. Walt's hallucinating
the dawn and then there's the water,
smacking slow then fast, like
good sex, bodies lost in the music.
Gulls swoop parabolas
to the rails' tangents. Mist
clouds Misery Island. Somewhere
out there he waits. Not Moby Dick,
not Ahab, not even Ishmael, but
the mad composer, harpooning
and being harpooned, salt tang
on his fevered tongue. Pirates still circle Java,
gun runners, smugglers. Whales, too,

though fewer. Poe's whirlpool
to the North. Iceberg. Death
has an etymology,
but no footnotes. Odysseus
was wrong: you don't bind yourself
and listen, you sing
and wait for an echo.

High Street Park

Whiff of gas near
the bike rack, glass

and dogshit in
the woodchips, the usual

"sucking" graffiti on the plastic slide.
On a black rubber seat, a note:

This is Megan's swing
You go, girl!

High Street Park: The Kindness of Boys

Two blocks from my house, tucked behind the homeless shelter, is High Street Park. It's an urban playground, with a typical, modest assortment of slides and structures set on an island of woodchips. The woodchips aren't the best material. Some get in children's shoes as they play, and some get scattered around the rest of the park. They litter the small asphalt loop circling the playground where my two boys used to ride their bikes, and they're sprinkled about the basketball court, which is annoying if you want to play basketball—though not as annoying as the broken glass.

When my sons were little, I'd walk them to High Street. It's where they learned to slide down poles, kick and throw balls, and ride bikes. It's where they would swing, and I would pretend to be a person walking, unaware, and get bumped by their feet as they swooshed forward. I'd spin and howl in mock pain, and they'd laugh and demand, "Again."

Some years back, before the city cracked down, the park was almost uninhabitable as the weather cooled. People would let their dogs shit in the woodchips, and they wouldn't clean it up. Too cool to decompose, and too warm to freeze and crumble, the turds just sat there for weeks. I spent a few visits frantically hopping in front of poop before my boys stepped in it, circumscribing the "safe" area.

It's not a lovable park, not clean or beautiful. Some might say it's not especially safe, given that it is set in the middle of a block, back from any streets, and that the homeless shelter, with its handful of documented child molesters, borders it.

And yet, it *is* beautiful. When my youngest son, Guthrie, was an infant, I would wheel him to the park, my other son, Aidan, three years old, walking beside us. When we would arrive, Guthrie would sit in his stroller, watching, as Aidan climbed the jungle gym. There would often be a few older boys about, and one of them, Frankie, would come over, lean down, and talk to Guthrie. He knew to use the high-pitched voice that babies love. Guthrie would listen and smile.

A few years later, when Aidan was into baseball, he and I would go to High Street and I'd pitch him whiffleballs on the basketball court, the park's only open space. He'd try to knock the ball over the chain link fence into a small parking lot. Sometimes Frankie and his friends, Jeff and Armando, all young teens, would join us, and we'd play a casual game of home run derby. Those boys would argue among themselves, but they were always kind to Aidan, always would tell him how good he was. The simple, encouraging words from older boys meant a lot to Aidan. I wonder if he even remembers them now.

The boy, Jeff, a skinny, dark-skinned Latino, was in an awful accident a couple years after those games. He and a friend had been riding a bike together, and they turned a corner and got hit by a truck. The accident was serious enough to make the local nightly news. Jeff got hit especially bad and had to be medevac-ed to Boston. I remember hearing the helicopter whirring over Salem that day and wondering what had happened.

I felt sick when I heard Jeff's name and realized who he was. I not only recalled the whiffleball, but a holiday concert at Horace Mann Elementary School. Jeff and my boys both attended Horace Mann, and when Aidan was in 2nd grade, Jeff was a 5th grader. At the end of one of the 5th grade's songs, Jeff scooted off the bleachers where the students were stacked and ran and slid on his knees across the stage, arms flung wide. It was a nice touch to the show by the school's music teacher, and Jeff was a perfect choice: graceful and ebullient. The younger children loved it.

Jeff had gone on to develop a love for basketball and real skill at playing it. He had made the Salem High varsity as a freshman in the winter before his accident.

His injuries were severe. Jeff was in the hospital a long time, and he was virtually paralyzed. The basketball program helped raise money so the family could get a wheelchair, a handicapped van, and a remodeled handicap-friendly bathroom. Now, three years later, Jeff is still unable to walk.

I know that Jeff is still in a wheelchair because I saw him at High Street Park recently. I had been at that park with Guthrie, now a seventh grader who likes basketball. Guthrie was taking shots and I was rebounding when a car pulled up and parked in the lot. Then another followed.

Four stocky, short guys got out, one bouncing a ball, and they started shooting around. Soon, a van pulled in, and two more guys got out and helped maneuver Jeff out the side door. They wheeled him over to the court and placed him just behind the basket, next to the pole that held it up.

And then these six guys, all about 20 years old, all a bit overweight, played three-on-three. They played hard, swearing at each other over fouls and the score, but they also played loose, friends who laughed at each other's screw-ups—a stupid, too-fancy pass, a humiliating blocked shot. Jeff laughed, too.

They weren't great players, but they weren't bad, their bodies a mix of grace and clunk. A few of them had sweet jump shots. Once or twice they even set picks for each other. I watched them between rebounding for Guthrie, and as I did, two things became clear: they were playing for fun, and they were playing for Jeff.

One March day well before Jeff's accident, back when Guthrie was still a little boy who liked playgrounds, he put on his coat and red-and-blue knit cap with the ties that dangled down around his chin, and I took him to High Street. There was a group of young teens, boys and girls, hanging out around the basketball courts. They were noisy—the boys making the girls squeal—and boisterous, shoving and pushing, an occasional swear, tossing woodchips at each other. They were teens, and, like many teens, they were mildly annoying and stupid. One of them, a tall blond boy with a bowl-shaped haircut, had made faces at me a few days earlier when I asked if Aidan and I could shoot at the same basket he and another boy were shooting at. Watching those teens, I thought—grumpily—how this was what Aidan would be enduring in the next few years as he headed into junior high.

Suddenly, there was a flurry of motion in the group, and they all crowded around something under the basketball net. "Oh, he's alive," I heard a girl say.

"Don't touch him," said another, "don't hurt him."

Then there were more squeals, and the crowd parted, and I saw the blond-haired boy with his hands cupped in front of him. He was holding a baby bird that had fallen out of its nest to the concrete. He looked up at the backboard, then stepped to the pole.

"Come here," he said to another boy. "Come here and hold it." The other boy came forward and put his hands out, and the blond boy eased the bird into the other's palms.

Then he climbed the pole, wrapping his arms and legs around it, pulling, and pulling again, until he was near the backboard and the nest that he must have seen somewhere on its back side. "Give him to me," the boy said, reaching one hand down. The other boy raised his cupped hands and the blond boy clutched the bird, lifted it up, and placed it in the nest. A girl clapped a little, the boy slid down the pole, and they all went back to being noisy.

Pretty soon Guthrie was ready to go, so we cut across the basketball court. I peeked up at the nest as we passed under the backboard. "Look at that," I said to Guthrie, "the baby bird is back in the nest." Then we ducked under the chain that kept cars from driving onto the playground and walked home. Maybe we even held hands.

No Heaven

The second floor of the Salem Senior Center, where the weekly Bingo game is held, feels as big and bright as heaven. The giant windows above our heads flood the room with sun. They are too high for us to see anything but the sky; no view of the disheveled graveyard on the eastern side. Rows of cardboard tables stretch across the expanse of floor. They seem small and squat, like thumbtacks on a huge bulletin board. The few elderly curled at those tables seem even smaller. Their slow movements seem even slower in proportion to the huge space. From above they must look like snails in a terrarium.

I had never been to a Bingo game, but my two neighbors, seventy-something sisters named Barbara and Bella, play here occasionally. It's down the block from where we live. The sisters aren't hardcore players; for them it's just one more senior center activity, like the bus trips to New York or Foxwoods (the gaming casino)—one more daub on their busy schedule.

I suspected the senior center game wasn't cutthroat, but social. Still, when I asked Barbara if people take it seriously, she emitted a high-pitched coo and said, "Some do." And when I arrived, the players seemed, well . . . experienced. Almost all of them had their own equipment—little metal ringed chips, knit holders for those chips, and a "wand," the brush-like magnet that sweeps over the cards after each game, clicking the chips up off the boards. And, of course, there were the lucky talismans. Bernie, the woman who oversaw the senior center game, had a penny with two tiny googly eyes glued onto it that she put in the free space of one of her boards.

Bernie played a lot of Bingo. After this game ended around 2:30 p.m., she was going to go home with her "friend," Arthur, a cheery bald man with glasses who helped distribute the money to the winners after each game. They would stay home for just fifteen minutes before going out to St. Joseph's for more Bingo. They would eat dinner at St. Joseph's, too, and wouldn't get back until 10 or 11 p.m.

Arthur was an anomaly; the players were almost entirely women. Out of 50 players—"exactly 50 today" said Bernie—there were six men. When things got a little noisy after someone had declared "Bingo," the caller would beg for quiet with the plea, "Ladies, ladies . . ."

Bernie did not use the word "ladies, but "girl." The "girl" who was a caller during the first half of the game also worked down at Salem Willows arcade in the "money cage." And Bernie took over this game when the "girl" who ran it got sick. "I was supposed to do it until she came back," Bernie said, "but she's six feet under." Bernie made a what-are-you-gonna-do face.

It was a face that she probably had to make a lot. Most of the players were in their 80s or 90s. "It's good for some of them that they just came here," Bernie said, and when the caller declared that the game to be played was "triple Bingo with two wilds," she pointed out, "this is a pretty complicated game for 90-year-olds." It was kind of complicated.

Before the games began, the talk was of money—the 15% senior discount at a clothing sale, how to get cheap movie tickets, how big the jackpots would be today—and food. Not only was I offered a gingerbread cookie when I sat down with some ladies (girls?) before the game, but Bernie stressed how good the dinners were at St. Joseph's, and she told me about the $2 lunch that was going on downstairs while we were playing—it was a "pretty nice-looking lunch," she said.

As the game was about to start, the maintenance man closed the blinds to make it easier to see the two televisions that display each ball after it pops up. No more sky; no more heaven, no hint of graveyard. One of the men let out a loud "Yee-hoo!," the caller reminded everyone of a rules change, and the game began. The talking stopped.

There is a certain basic fascination to the game. One watches the cards fill up, patterns taking shape and disappearing, the way one might watch rain make paths down a window. One notes the oddnesses—that's three "I"s in a row, "71" hasn't come up once all day—as if they might hold a secret, as if there might be a reason behind the randomness. And, of course, there is the thrill of victory. The opportunity to win the four-dollar twenty-five cent pot keeps your eyes moving from the televisions to the cards in front of you.

There is also something soothing about the game's rhythms. It's simple and quiet, like meditation. The caller's voice repeating the number twice, the hands floating over cards, dropping a chip here or there. And in between games, the lovely clacking of chips as they leap onto wands and are shed into the personalized holders.

Yet, ultimately, over the course of the two-and-a-half hours I was there, I came to realize an incredibly sad fact: Bingo is boring. It's not like chess, or poker, or even rock, paper, scissors; there is no strategy, no challenge. If it "keeps your mind sharp," as one of the ladies told me, it's a butter-knife sharp. One follows directions, and one might win. One will probably lose.

When it was over, and I walked through the sunny parking lot down the leaf-strewn street to my house, a question arose, a question I'm not sure I have the right to ask, but which I will ask anyway: why do so many people choose to spend so much of their last few years of life playing this game?

Perhaps they play Bingo because they are dying (we're all dying!), and the simplemindedness of the game—the fact that it is only about fate—seems to mirror how they view their lives, and the inevitability of death. What are you gonna do? Someday your number will come up—Bingo! You're dead!

But that seems to make Bingo a game for the morbid, and perhaps it is the flip side of the game—the fact that it is a *game*—that makes it attractive. If you are still able to hear the caller well enough to know the number and letter, if your eyes are still strong enough to spot the digits on your cards, your fingers still nimble enough to drop the chips quickly and accurately, then you are still in the game. Bingo is a reminder that you are still alive.

Or is it the competitiveness? Some last chance to beat other humans, to feel that you are blessed, on top of the heap, to believe that you still can be president (even if you are a woman). After one game, Bernie commented on the winner: "Joyce is so lucky." Was I imagining it, or did I hear a tinge of jealousy in her observation?

Maybe not. Maybe the game was, like the room it was played in, appealing because it was a version of heaven. There is one voice that people attend to—the caller, whose pronouncements reverberate throughout the cavernous space. Unlike on earth, God's words have little ambiguity. There aren't even words, which would require interpretation. The world, or language, at least, has been broken down to its most basic elements: numbers and letters. God commands G54, and the dutiful angels cover square G54 on their holy charts. Nothing could be simpler, or more just. There is no argument over the text. No strategizing, no plotting, no way to know God's will but to listen and to look. The mind is at bay. There is no evil here.

Salem Common on Training Day, 1808

—a painting by George Ropes, Jr.

The elm trees rise up like flames.
They line the Common,
dwarfing the regiments and
their puny flags—red and white.

The soldiers are too far away
to see clearly—some red blurs,
some blue. Phalanxes.
No one is watching. The families

and children and wagons
and horses in the foreground
seem to pass slowly in front
of the elms. In the middle distance,

shadowy, a brown mass
of citizens surrounds
some political speaker.
Everyone, save

the strolling civilians
and their leaping dogs,
is inside the white fence
that borders the Common.

The republic is thirty-two years old.
No planes, of course, in the sky, just
specks of gulls, and dirty
cotton ball clouds. The elms,

not yet destroyed by disease,
seem like they are trying to hold
back the sunset, which explodes
orange at the tips of their leaves.

Two Voices from the Trials

Samuel Wardwell

If I really could tell fortunes, you'd think I would have foreseen this night, this cell. I would have heard the news from Salem and known it would spread, as it is spreading, across the colony. I heard the afflicted girls have been invited to Gloucester, and to my town, Andover.

But I did this to myself. I belied myself. And I'm going to the gallows, whether I own it or no, so hear me: I lied. I lied. I am no wizard. I made no pact with a black man in my fields twenty years ago. I told that story because I hoped it might set me free. And those good women I said were witches, too—I regret smearing their name.

What is evil, what transgression? Yes, I told fortunes for sport, but no devil aided me. I liked to study a person, to see what they would reveal. And yes, I am a Quaker, and I married a widow said to be above my class. But these are not signs of the devil . . . .

I took her daughter in, she accepted my son, and we had five more children together . . . . Now, they've tricked my wife and daughter to bely themselves as I did. While we sit in jail, my children are being dispersed across Andover—to those houses of my neighbors who watched me get carted away. Who will tell my children the truth about me if I could not even tell the truth about myself? Will you?

Mary Eastey

Two months ago, they hanged my sister, Rebecca. This man right here led her past me. And then he charged her family for her shackles. See how he stands there, devoid of mercy. It was just so in July, when he led my dear Rebecca away. She clutched my hand then, this same hand I hold out to you.

All because, six years ago, my husband testified against the Putnams for cutting and taking trees that weren't theirs. And so they testified against me and my sisters, cutting down lives not theirs. And some were inclined to believe them, rousing scurrilous accusations from twenty years ago against my own mother.

But we are beyond recriminations now. I know I must die, and my appointed time is set. Tomorrow I cross the North River for the last time. Part of me rejoices that my earthly trials draw to an end. Do you see how they keep us? Chained, the stench of dung and tobacco. I, an upstanding citizen, like my sister, respected in my church, my family. All seven of my children will be there tomorrow.

No, I am looking forward. Not for me, but for you—for you I pray that no more innocent blood be shed. By my own innocence, I know that those who judge are in the wrong way. And I beg them to please examine those afflicted persons carefully, and keep them apart some time, and try some of these confessing witches. I am confident several of them have belied themselves and others. Should you do this, I am certain you shall see an alteration of these things, and our community will better know the will of the Lord. And the future shall be brighter than the present dark days.

The Great Fire

Commemoration

The intersection of Proctor, Boston, and Bridge Streets in Salem, Massachusetts, is drab. A Dunkin Donuts spreads its pink and beige cheer; there's an empty fenced-in lot with a coating of rubble, a three-family brick building, and a Walgreens, fringed with a parking lot. It's an area no one has bothered to spruce up; the businesses will do their business regardless. Even the roads seem uncared for. The steady traffic on Boston Street must negotiate some jagged potholes.

I stopped at this spot one day when I was out on a jog, drawn by a waist-high boulder in the corner of the Walgreens' lot, sitting like an island in a pond of wood chips. On the side facing the intersection was a brown plaque. Bordered in gold with gold lettering, the plaque read:

> *At 1:37 PM on June 25, 1914, Box 48 was pulled for a fire in the Korn Leather Factory on this site at number 57 Boston Street in an area of town known as Blubber Hollow, followed at 1:41 PM by a general alarm.*
>
> *This was the start of the Great Salem Fire.*
>
> *This memorial is dedicated to those brave firefighters from Salem and surrounding communities who fought that conflagration.*

The words were accompanied by an image of a fire alarm box, a bolded "48" on it.

I'd heard of the Great Salem Fire. It had destroyed a third of the city, burning 1,376 buildings and leaving over 15,000 homeless in a population of 48,000. It had been national news, on the front pages of *The Boston Globe* and *The New York Times* for several days. The Saturday after the fire, it was estimated that up to half-a-million spectators traipsed through the smoky aftermath. Photos record these visitors strolling down a decimated Lafayette Street, one of Salem's most stately boulevards, the black remnants of trees and an occasional brick husk of a building rising from the ground behind them.

I looked around. There wasn't anything that made me think of the fire, although just up the hill to the right, a place the fire hadn't reached, I noticed a long, windowless building that seemed to have once been a factory.

Behind the monument, a large sign for Walgreens sat on a sturdy brick rectangular base. Unlike the plaque, these words were visible from the street:

PEPSI 2LTR 4/$5

DORITOS 2/$4.29

GET YOUR FLU SHOT HERE TODAY

On the sidewalk nearby, a yellow fire hydrant, and near that, between Boston Street and the monument, a telephone pole, a gray utility box, and a skinny red fire alarm box as tall as a person. I wondered (it couldn't be!) if the box was the same one that was pulled during the fire. It was so old and beat up, the paint faded and peeling. If I pulled the alarm's white handle, would anything happen?

Despite the fire's thorough destruction, it seems a footnote in this city saturated with history. Salem was the first capital of the Massachusetts Bay Colony, the home of the country's first millionaire. It was a great shipping capital in the New World, and the grand mansions of the ship owners still line stately Chestnut Street, though some have been divided into condos. Nathaniel Hawthorne is its reluctant native son. His House of Seven Gables is an historical attraction that looks out into the Atlantic, just across the street from Ye Olde Pepper Companie, the nation's oldest candy store. And then there are the Witch Trials.

Amidst all this, the fire is an afterthought, something that some people know about, but which has not ensconced itself in Salem's museum of memory.

I turned to the plaque and ran my fingers over the raised lettering. How do you commemorate a disaster? The words felt dull to me. A fact about when the fire started, and then a bland one-sentence acknowledgment of the firefighters. Of course they are "brave."

It seemed obvious that this plaque was written well after the fact, after the smoke had not just cleared, but had been forgotten. If it wasn't for the striking name, "Blubber Hollow," which refers to the nineteenth-century practice of using whale blubber to tan leather, the memorial would be as dull as the rest of the intersection, something you pass because you must.

It turns out that, yes, the plaque was put up in 1964, to mark the 50th anniversary of the fire.

I imagine the dedication: a couple city officials and some corralled staff members, a local historian, a few firefighters required to attend, all standing awkwardly at the intersection for 15 minutes. *Can we go home now?*

The words are a challenge, almost a taunt from those who wrote them, who set the boulder here: *We, who commemorated this, had no idea what to say. What have you got?*

*

Despite its impact at the time, the fire didn't merit a chapter in *Salem: Place, Myth, and Memory*, an anthology of essays on the city. The book's editors write that "Commemoration privileges some events over others, even when those others have touched a greater number of lives more profoundly . . . even dramatic local occurrences can lack the cachet of an enshrining event: in local catastrophes, lives may be lost, but the story of their death yields no moral."

For me, too, the fire meant little to the Salem I knew. My ancestor, Mary Towne Eastey, was killed for being a witch. Another, Thomas Perkins, sat on the jury that found her guilty. The legacy of the Witch Trials is inescapable. My other connection to Salem has been through teaching at the local university, Salem State, a career that has made me aware of the gulf of class in education. My students often work outside of school as much as I do at school. My wife and I raised our two sons here and live a few blocks from downtown; I spent a decade coaching them in Salem's Little League, where I encountered a cross-section of the city's boys. Fire? What fire?

The fire did make a brief appearance in a long sequence of poems that I wrote about Salem, "Montage of Brick and Water," but perhaps it's in those poems more than I realized. The city seems filled with brick, and some of that brick, which the poems treat as a sign of age, was probably a sign of the rebuilding. Brick fills the downtown commercial district, an area that didn't go up in flames. And—I've been told—brick lies between the inner and outer walls of my house, built in 1916, to help limit destruction in the case of another fire. Though I've never seen that brick, I like knowing (or believing) that it's there. I credit it for keeping things temperate; cooler in the summer, warmer in the winter. It makes our lives more livable.

We know the basement of my house, at 48 Winthrop Street, has the old fieldstone foundation from the previous house. In heavy rains or snows, water seeps in, sometimes several inches. When it floods like this, my wife puts on her boots and putters with the pump, while I scurry about in the rain, yank the hose through the basement window, and pull it to the gutter. We've become accustomed to this. "If you live in Salem, you're going to get water in your basement," a lifelong resident told us. Perhaps those floods are the past, reappearing every so often. Perhaps they've come to put out a fire.

When I dig in my puny yard, trying to level the topsoil or to add a plant, the earth always yields something that says fire: shards of pottery, dulled pieces of glass, or blackened soil that seem the remains of some long-ago wooden house. Once, I found a rusted pair of scissors, another time an old spoon.

My backyard has grass and some flowers now, but for most of my first two decades in Salem, it was a small, enclosed slab of packed dirt. My boys grew up playing in it, pitching and batting foam balls for hours, running the few feet from one base to another. I spent a lot of time out there, too. We didn't think about what was pushing up from the ground, the bits of the past. The flitting ball of the present held our attention, drew us forward into our joys, our lives.

Now, I look out my back window, beyond my own yard, at my neighbors' roofs and think about fragility and time and what lies beneath us, how Broad Street Cemetery, just up the block, stopped some destruction, the fire unable to leap the grass and stones. That night, as the flames were brought under control, those made homeless slept in the cemetery, and, reports say, a child was born there.

Conflagration

In the shadow of Gallows Hill, at the foot of Proctor's Ledge, where the accused were hanged in 1692, the Korn Leather Factory blew, and the fire began.

It shot up the south side of Boston Street, wiping out a few neighborhoods directly to the south, where Splaine Little League field is, where Hawthorne Plaza is with its CVS and auto parts store. The firefighters dynamited ten houses on Boston Street to slow the blaze, but it only sped the destruction, the rubble catching fire. Though the fire did cross Boston

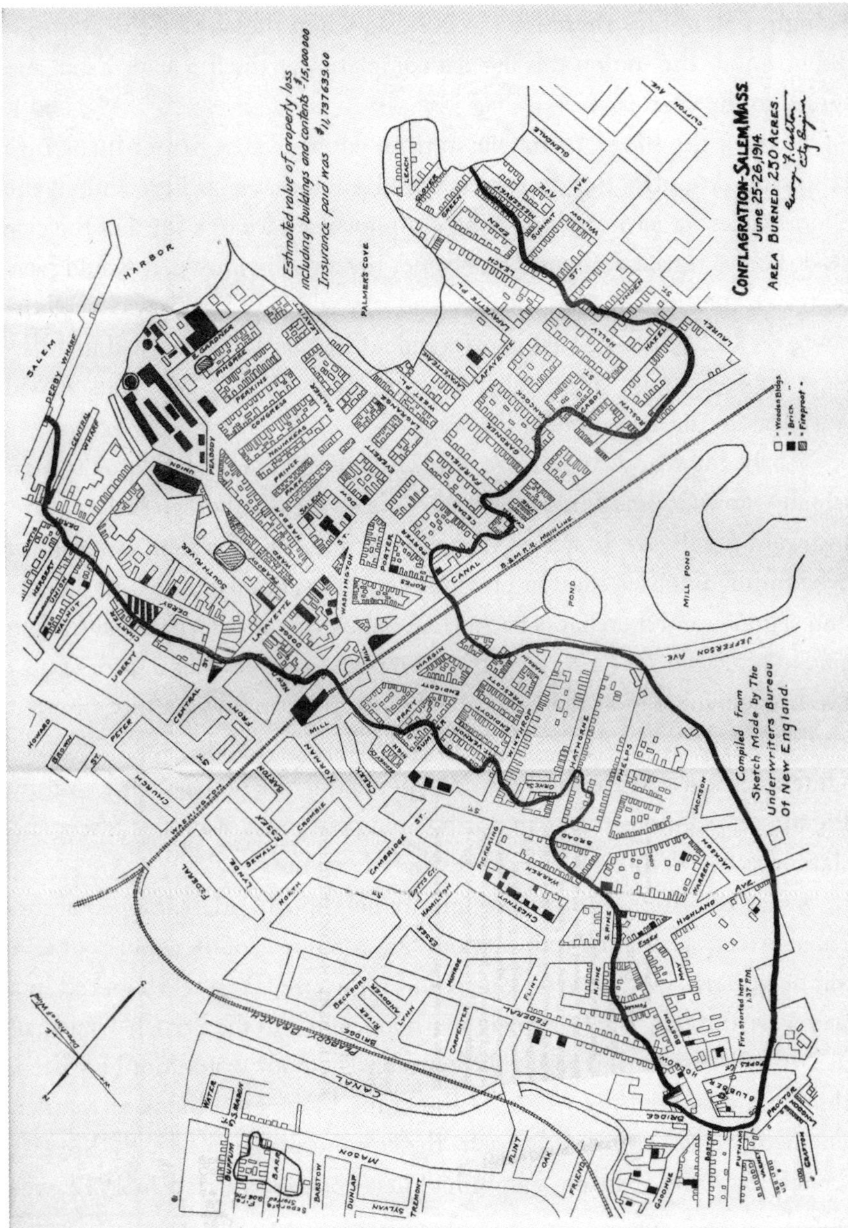
Conflagration - Salem, Mass.
June 25-26, 1914.
Area Burned 250 Acres.
Estimated value of property loss including buildings and contents $15,000,000
Insurance paid was $11,737,633.00
Compiled from Sketch Made by The Underwriters Bureau of New England.
Salem Harbor
Derby Wharf
Palmer's Cove
Mill Pond
Pond
Canal
B. & M. R.R. Main Line
Peabody Branch
Fire started here 1.37 P.M.
Wooden Bldgs.
Brick
Fireproof

Street in places, the wind, or something, kept it from traveling north until after it crossed Essex Street.

On the corner of Essex and Boston was a fire station, and some people brought belongings there for safekeeping when they heard the alarm. It did no good. The station was burned completely as the fire leapt Essex and spread to the northeast.

Just up the block from the station, where Essex Street turns into Highland Ave., the fire destroyed the Highland Ave. bridge and all the phone cables underneath, knocking out phone service to a third of the city. Had the fire traveled down Essex Street toward downtown, it would have destroyed the city's business district, and it would have likely swallowed the house on 292 Essex, a house of Alexander Graham Bell, who had first displayed his telephone in the Salem Lyceum back in 1877: "Mr. Watson, will you speak to the audience?"

At the Highland Ave. bridge, the fire couldn't get up the hill to the high school—now Collins Middle School—and so it rushed down Jackson Ave. and went northeast. It spared Chestnut Street, where Salem's wealthiest lived in huge houses that, in previous centuries, had belonged to Salem's ship captains and merchants back when Salem was an international trading hub. In his book, *The Salem Fire,* firefighter Arthur Jones tells a story of how two homeowners used tea kettles and pans to tamp down a roof fire that would likely have led to Chestnut Street burning, but it also seems like firefighters made a stand around this area, protecting the homes of the wealthy. The fire veered more east than north wiping out most of Phelps Street and Hathorne and Winthrop, the street where I live now.

Once the fire had shot through my neighborhood, it hopped across Canal Street, skirted the train station, and expanded south, wiping out several neighborhoods between Canal and Lafayette. Then it whooshed in a fiery wave through The Point neighborhood, home to the French-Canadian factory workers, until it reached the water. The poor would not be spared. The fire incinerated the whole of The Point, block after block of wooden tenement houses converted to ash. The community's majestic St. Joseph's French Catholic Church, which had just been completed in 1912, was gutted.

Despite the destruction, there were only three casualties. One, a Civil War veteran named Withey, lived just across the street from where our house is now, on the corner of Winthrop and Prescott. As the fire leapt across the rooftops and the sirens blew out the city's eardrums, the Marshall told the old veteran to leave his house, to leave the heavy chest of remembrances—medals, folded uniforms—and hurry to the safety of the grassy cemetery. What would you save? Withey said no. The door closed, the lock clicked, and the Marshall stood on the porch, fingered his gun, then walked to the next house.

Out my window, almost directly across the street, I see the small house, built on the site of Withey's last stand. It's sky blue with white trim.

*

Seeing his car on fire, a man leapt into it and drove it into the ocean, where it burned down to the waterline.

Firemen sat in puddles from their spray, recovering from the intense heat.

Among the 60 injured were some who jumped from the second floor of the Korn Factory, and a fire captain who was "hit in the face by flying nozzles."

Militia clearing neighborhoods in the path of the fire found three babies abandoned in houses.

Three days after the fire, sidewalks in the burned area were still too hot to walk on.

*

Handing out flyers for the Salem Arts Festival one summer, I talk with a cop who is directing traffic. Next to us is one of the hundreds of fire alarm boxes, like the one on the corner where the fire started. It's plastered with bumper stickers for local bands. "Do these things still work?" I ask. "Yeah, they do," he tells me, but no one ever uses them.

They worked in 1914, sending out the news quickly. For what must have been chaos, it all seemed so organized. Even though there were moments of confusion among the firefighters, and the water pressure prevented them from adequately holding the fire off in many places, and the dynamiting strategy didn't work, they reacted quickly and with purpose. Firefighters from the neighboring town of Peabody were on the scene within 20 minutes, and several other towns sent help swiftly. Alarms rang, and people managed to get out of their houses, though they didn't have time and help to remove many valuable belongings. Such efficiency seems like it would be hard to duplicate today, even in this era of cell phones and instant news. How many now would just shrug and say, *I'll wait and see what happens.*

At 2:00 p.m., about 23 minutes after the fire began, the Mayor declared martial law. The militia swooped in before the fire was put out, and there was almost no looting, at least no documented looting. Their orders: "Shoot to kill."

The greatest loss of life came later that evening. A few blocks from Blubber Hollow, in another leather factory, another container of celluloid exploded, and a fire raged that took out two blocks, including some stables. Thirteen horses were killed. That fire would have been known as a major fire in Salem history, had it not been for what had happened earlier that day, and it would have been much more disastrous had the fire crews from around the North Shore not been in the city, battling the original blaze.

In the recollections of the fire, this smaller fire is an afterthought, and the horses get a sentence. It hurts to imagine their terror, the frenzy inside the stables, kicking at their gates, braying into the smoky night. At some point they must have known, as people know, that they were doomed.

*

In a photo taken from the height of the high school—now Collins Middle School—one can see the totality of the destruction: the roads laid out like maps, with little in between them except ash. The black and white photo is mostly white, indicating the grey ash, but there are chimneys, rising out of the white like so many fingers, or blades of grass. For blocks, only chimneys and char. It looks somewhat like an athletic field, a setting for some alien game. Of course, it looks like a war-ravaged city, too.

I think of the difference between wood and brick.

Photos are the primary remembrance of the fire; they make it most real. In the Salem State University Archives are hundreds of photos of the fire and its aftermath. A handful of books exist about the fire, but the fire has been preserved mostly in images. The recent book, *The Great Salem Fire of 1914: Images From the Phillips Library Collection*, is largely photos. They are breathtaking, and they document the thoroughness of the devastation, particularly when paired with photos of Salem before the fire. Pre-fire, Lafayette Street's stately elms and broad thoroughfare reflect Salem's past wealth. Post-fire, the street is thronged with tourists walking or driving their boxy cars through a landscape similar to Dresden or Hiroshima.

And yet, the photos only touch so much. Many of them were created for commercial appeal. Most of the memorable images of the fire were made into postcards, which were mailed across the country as souvenirs. They emphasized the drama of disaster. The canny didn't hesitate to make money on misfortune.

An ad in *The Boston Globe* on June 27, two days after the fire:

GREAT SALEM FIRE
POSTCARDS and prints for framing now ready; big money for hustlers.
Agents wanted. Samples on receipt of 15c.
TICHNOR BROS. Inc, 151 Causeway St., Boston

I looked at two photos that open *The Great Salem Fire*. One is of children looking expectantly as a circus comes to town two days before the fire, peering from behind a rope down the street at the unseen parade. The second is of a group of children made homeless by the fire, getting food at a refugee camp. At first, I thought that the more haggard children in the second photo seemed more like children of Salem today, and perhaps that's true, but really, in both photos the children seemed fundamentally different, as if from an alien culture. In the first photo, they are all dressed up, their faces full and round. They look like munchkins. Frankly, they are a bit frightening. In the other photo the faces are more gaunt and less clean, smudged with dirt, and they stare directly at the camera. They look like children of the Dust Bowl.

In another image, a postcard, are five men, three seated, four hatted, in front of a black gate rimming a cemetery. The writing in white letters across the bottom says: *Our Cook House, Salem Fire June 25, 1914.* In front of the men, a stack of firewood, a big drum, several large rectangular containers.

Most likely, this was a place where food was prepared as part of the relief effort.

I know that black gate. It's at the end of my block, the cemetery next to the senior center with the ancient, broken headstones, the one where the baby was born.

Community

Some months after the fire, Montanye Perry, a fiction writer and past director of a night school for immigrants, wrote a series of articles on the relief efforts for the main Salem newspaper, *The Salem Evening News*. These were collected in a thin book, *The Salem Fire Relief*. Her stated purpose, laid out on the opening page, was to "furnish an inquiring public" with details about the relief effort. There had been complaints. Some were that a few "imposters" collected relief that they were not entitled to, and some were that the relief efforts were inefficient, caught up in red tape and squabbling.

While the articles freely admitted to such problems, they argued, via moralistic episodes with unidentified characters ("the Doctor," "Business Man," and "Wealthy Citizen") that the distribution was fair, the red tape necessary, and the fraud infrequent. The articles pointed out that human nature was such that people would want what others had, and even noted that a freeloader's desire to game the system wasn't so different than a businessman's desire to corner a market. The articles' spirit is triumphant, noting informal help, such as rich citizens lending cars and time for those made homeless, relief workers and doctors volunteering for weeks, and the anonymous person who pinned ten dollars to the swaddling of a refugee baby. They credited the militia, which established and kept order in the camps the first two weeks after the fire.

Still, throughout the book, there is an acknowledgment that people were disgruntled about the recovery. The book closes on an odd note. "Let those whose faith in humanity has been shaken by the events of these trying weeks take heart." The "calamity" may have "brought to light some glaring defects in human nature," but it also "revealed glorious heights of generosity and powers of self-sacrifice." And, in her final paragraph, Perry says that the story may seem to "present a mass of crude, sordid ugliness," but, taking the long view, the "picture is far from being a discouraging commentary on the human race in its entirety."

*

These undercurrents of class conflict and prejudice come to light when tracing the reasons for the fire's extensive damage. Franklin Wentworth, a Salem councilman in the years before the fire, wrote that Salem "assumed no responsibility to protect the lives and livelihood of her common people, and her property-owning class was content to run its daily risk because it knew it could saddle its fire losses upon the country."

In 1910, Wentworth, responding to a report from the National Board of Fire Underwriters, tried to pass a roof policy for Salem, which would have required noncombustible roofs on all structures. The city council rejected it, viewing it as a scam of the insurance industry. Likewise, it was recommended that high-pressure pumps be purchased, but the city didn't want to invest the 150,000 dollars that it would have required. In a rare exhibition of personality, the firefighter Arthur Jones writes in his account that "Someone good at figures could figure out how long it took to burn $150,000.00 on June 25th." Recalling the fire, Orille L'Heureux told how his father tried to wet down the house, but that there was no water pressure, as if the hose was simply peeing.

The Korn Leather Factory was also at fault. In cutting corners, it put workers at risk (and, it turns out, the whole city). According to a state official, "if the factory had been equipped with a sprinkler system . . . there was nothing in this building which water would not have extinguished." After the fire, factory owner Max Korn had to rebuild in Peabody, the next town over, because of threats in Salem.

*

Stories of disasters often include babies. A living baby represents survival of the species, and an investment by humans in the future—it's worth it to bring new life into the world. That baby born at the Broad Street Cemetery? It shows endurance, continuation. Robert Withey, the Civil War vet down the street, has his life extinguished in the fire; a new soul appears that night on the same block among the long dead.

Jones' book describes the babies born at the maternity hospital in the week after the fire: "three French, one Italian, and one American." Distinctions were made.

Those babies rumored abandoned in the tenements? In the media, their story might reinforce prejudices against the poor—what kind of people abandon infants? But is there also a hint at a desperation in some immigrants' lives, perhaps the unspoken wishes of a few overwhelmed women. Maybe we want to start over, or at least have a break. One baby was found with a simple note in Forest River Park: "Tecla. Gone to Brockton."

What to make of Selma Florence Barstol, who took her parents in when fire took their home, even though she was about to give birth? Shortly after her baby was born, she died, and *The Salem Evening News* blamed "the excitement of the fire and misfortune of her parents" for her death. The baby survives, but the fire extracted its price—thus kindness is rewarded.

And then there was the French-speaking woman who went to the maternity hospital, distraught. Despite the language barrier, it was finally understood that she had been separated from her eight-month-old baby. He was found the next day at the North Shore Children's Hospital, where he had been given the name "Shackles."

*

It took me a month of poking through books, returning again and again to the map, blowing up the map online, walking, jogging, and biking, simply to get a handle on the fire's borders. I'd traverse the city, testing: "this block burned, this one didn't." A map makes things look so clear and tidy, but when you live in a place, and walk its streets, the forest can disappear in the trees.

One February day, I biked through The Point neighborhood, which runs about a half mile from Lafayette Street to the water. The city was drying out from a cold rain, sunny and 40 degrees, and I was thankful for the biking gloves I'd gotten for Christmas. At the time of the fire, The Point had been home to French Canadian laborers. It's now home to Salem's more recent immigrants from the Dominican.

After the fire, the shell of the grand St. Joseph's French Catholic Church, built out of brick and stone, seemed like the only raised structure in The Point. Between the two remaining towers, a 12-foot statue of a hirsute St. Joseph rose over what had been the entrance, some 100 feet above ground. For the next thirty years, the statue hovered in the neighborhood sky. It was taken down and interred on the site in 1944 in a public ceremony. Families photographed their children beside it before it was lowered into the earth.

The French-Canadian community, decimated by the fire, struggled to raise funds to build a new church. Governor Walsh, speaking to a huge crowd of refugees at Forest River Park on June 28th, promised funds for "an even more beautiful edifice." This didn't come to pass. For many years the parish made do, renovating the basement of the destroyed church to hold masses, building a rectory and school on the site, until, finally, a new church was completed in 1954. That church was shut down in 2004, during the church closings after the priest sexual abuse scandal, and, in 2013, it was razed to make way for new housing and businesses. St. Joseph, who had become little more than a rumor, was unearthed during that construction, and, in a small private ceremony, was reinterred beneath Jimmy John's Pizza and the Lafayette Apartments, while, in the surrounding neighborhood where French had been spoken and sung, Spanish filled the air.

In 2017, Salem held a ballot referendum on whether to declare itself a sanctuary city. The sound and fury of the opposition signified something—discomfort with the browning of Salem, the fact that in The Point, a few square blocks of the city, more Spanish was heard than English, or that a woman buying groceries in Market Basket might not understand the cashier (or vice versa) and slow the line. It was a time when the Trump administration was threatening various measures on cities that passed such resolutions, including withholding federal funds. Reports were coming out about children being separated from their parents when they requested asylum at the border. Now, in 2024, Trump's rhetoric has only gotten harsher as he ramps up his campaign, and, despite the scrubbing of a lot of politics from Facebook, my feed gets the occasional ugly meme about the need for a wall, or how "our" country isn't "ours" anymore.

*

I biked down Congress, past Celia's Spanish Cuisine, looked both ways off the wide street down narrow ones, which seemed even narrower because of the crowded three and four-deckers that were separated by spaces not more than an arm's length, and sometimes by no space at all. There were no front yards or back yards, not even a scrim of dirt or grass between sidewalk and street. The neighborhood appeared similar to what it looked like at the time of the fire: crowded, treeless, except now the buildings were made of brick, not wood. Now, though, there is the occasional mural on the side of a brick building, a splash of vibrant color.

In a corner of The Point, at the baseball field at Palmer Cove, I turned left past Harbor Sweets, a candy shop. The most expensive chocolate in America, the founder proudly proclaimed. Though locals shop there, its thriving mail order business made it successful. It felt odd, yet oddly right, here among the tenements; both seemed from another century.

Then, I went into Shetland Office Park on the waterfront, an area that, before and after the fire, had housed the Naumkeag Steam Cotton Factory. The factory made cotton sheets, and it was a major employer of the French-Canadian immigrants. The factory—all Salem's factories—are long gone, though these buildings, built after the fire, remain. I passed the Bureau of Deeds and warehouses for self-storage, then the Salem Academy Charter School, and the Department of Transitional Assistance.

I looped back up Congress, then turned down some of the narrow streets and passed a woman hurrying out of a car and into a house, wearing a leopard skin nightgown. A few houses down, a sketchy man loitered on the sidewalk, scoping things out. Then past the house where my son's friend lived, the one he used to jam with in the Music Department's practice rooms at Salem State.

What exactly was I looking for? Traces of a 100-year-old fire? Or was it something simpler, something in the present that could make meaning of the past? I think I was searching for community.

Eventually, I got beyond the reach of the fire, moving toward my stomping grounds: Forest River Park and Salem State University. I know both well. They are Salem to me, as much as any place, and both survived the flames. My work life revolves around teaching at the University, and I spent a decade of summers on the Little League field at Forest River, shouting instructions to children, my own and others: "Cover the bag," "Head on the ball." Evenings were communal gatherings, the field's lights bleeding into the night of the surrounding neighborhood. Spanish and English in the aluminum bleachers and in the dugouts. Children lining up at the snack bar.

I may know Salem best through its baseball fields. It is where I'm closest to its ground, where it's flat, or flattened, with no buildings, like the city after the fire. I can even imagine the cooled ash like the Forest River infield dirt after a long dry spell, powdery and dusty, kicked up into puffy clouds by a bored eight-year-old second baseman.

*

The largest and longest standing refugee camp was established at Forest River. It housed over 1500 refugees, who lived in rows and rows of white tents. The 400 tents had wooden floors, which made life a bit more bearable when the rains came. Though the tents were identical, the refugees soon put their names or other markers in front of their lodgings to distinguish them, and simply to help them find their way back to their temporary homes.

The camp was established by the militia, and it functioned like a small village. It had mess halls, an infirmary, a post office, and church services. Mass, in French, was held at the end of every day. At first, a military bugle called the refugees to mass. Later, the pastors used a large bell to gather their parishioners.

The Red Cross had both paid and unpaid nurses, and doctors from the area donated their time. Volunteers distributed food and clothing. Children's clothing was especially needed. The volunteers came from across the country, many with experience in recovery after disasters. A long list of items provided to a "Mrs. Bik" from the Salem Relief Committee includes a stove, a dining table and chairs, an icebox, a sewing machine, four pillows, a double bed and bedding, other various furniture, including a crib, 50 dollars in cash, 62 dollars for food, 12 dollars for rent, and "clothing for woman and three children." At the end of the account is the sentence, "The law provides that Mothers' Aid shall be adequate!" complete with exclamation point.

A local band played concerts at Forest River, the refugees singing along to "patriotic airs," whether it was "La Marseillaise," "The Maple Leaf Forever," or "The Star-Spangled Banner." While there were strong distinctions and prejudices of class and culture (think of those un-American babies), the community seemed to accept its diversity, as heard in the sermons of the time. Dewitt Clark, of the Tabernacle Congregational Church, noted how many sufferers "were not of the American type." "In seeking to do acts of kindness and goodness," Clark noted, "lines had been obliterated and all were one people." And Henry Bolinger, at St. Peter's Episcopal Church, praised the city's "great spirit of kindness and sympathy . . . out of it will come something better, something more lasting."

*

I circled Forest River, stopping to check out a wreath with a red bow and gold bells that had been left on one of the benches facing Salem Harbor. I passed a man jogging with his dog, a woman walking hers, and when I biked up to the playground, found a mother and two young girls.

When my boys were little, I'd take them to this tree-dotted high ground beyond the parking area, the baseball field out of view. Aidan, my oldest, loved to play on the wooden cars. He'd scoot into the driver's seat and tell me to get in beside him. I would, though I'd have to sit on the divider between the front seat and the back, and we would go "shopping." When we would get to the "store," he'd climb out and gather rocks and sticks, pretending they were all sorts of foods. He'd put them in the back of the car, and off we'd go, moving only through time.

When the boys were a bit older, we'd take them to the huge wading pool in the opposite corner of the park from the ballfield. There was a large black witch painted on the bottom, the Salem High mascot. On hot summer days, the pool filled with Salem's children, especially those from The Point, those who couldn't afford the Y. It was a gathering place for community. The children—pink, cream, brown and black—clambered over each other, shouting and laughing, despite the occasional fight or injury. The parents set up towels in the shade, drifting into the pool now and then to soak in the cool.

*

Closer to home—my home—is Bertram Field, which was the site of the other main refugee camp. The French Canadians burned out of The Point went the mile south to Forest River; the other refugees—Polish, Greeks, Eastern European Jews—ended up at Bertram. The Jews insisted on their own area and a kosher cook.

Bertram Field sits on the raised hill beside what was then the high school, now Collins Middle School. My two sons used to walk the six blocks to Collins, the reverse route of the fire. Then they went to Salem High, in a time when middle-class white families fled the public schools, a time when, although Salem is over three-quarters white, Salem's schools shifted from being majority white to Latino.

In a photo of Bertram after the fire, the football field's bleachers rise behind the line of tents. From Bertram's hill, you could look down across the ruins, the lonely smokestacks in the rubble, those fingers reaching from the ground, accusing the sky.

Now, although the field is still there—it's where the high school plays its football games—it's fringed by woods. The middle schoolers, no doubt, sneak into these trees for their first tastes of pot or sex, the unregulated shade a first step into life's wildness. And now, it has become increasingly a hangout for the unhoused, who have found their way up from Boston and planted a few tents out of view from the neighborhood's backyards.

*

In the camps, those with power exercised it on those with less. Captain Blanchard took a reporter on a stroll through Forest River in early July, and when he found men who weren't working, he'd interrogate them as to why, threatening them with removal from camp if they weren't at work in the future.

Assertions of power were justified as efforts to prevent sloth, and sometimes, for the sake of public health and cleanliness. At Forest River Park, Arthur Tremblay's attempt to sell beer was shut down for being against "liquor laws." An account in *The Salem Evening News* describes officers ordering "some youngster" to pick up "rubbish." At Bertram Field's camp, a child was taken from his parents, against their will, and brought to the contagious hospital when he had tonsillitis. In despair, or protest, the mother left— "she got past the guards at the gate and wandered out into the darkness, where for a time she was lost."

Commemoration

When the smoke hadn't yet cleared, when the smell of it still lingered over the rebuilt railroad tracks, in the firefighters' gear, in the frazzled minds of Salem's citizens, the fire still had meaning. In 1915, on the one-year anniversary, a plaque was installed in Lafayette Park. The park itself was one of several created after the conflagration to prevent a fire from crossing the city so rapidly, so easily. Triangular, the park borders The Point. Park and plaque sit across the street from where St. Joseph's Church burned to the ground.

IN COMMEMORATION
OF THE
ENTERPRISE AND RESOLUTE SPIRIT
WITH WHICH
SALEM AROSE FROM HER ASHES
LOOKED CALAMITY IN THE FACE
AND REBUILT HER WALLS,
ON THIS SPOT
IN THE PATHWAY OF THE GREAT FIRE OF
JUNE 25, 1914,
WHICH SWEPT FROM THE WEST
TO THE WATER'S EDGE
DESTROYING ABOUT ONE THIRD
OF THE CITY
AND RENDERING HOMELESS
MORE THAN ONE THIRD OF
HER PEOPLE
THIS TABLET WAS ERECTED
BY
J. ACKERMAN COLES, M.D., L.L.D.
1915

The city rededicated the plaque and gussied it up in 2014 to commemorate the 100th anniversary, but I doubt that, other than for that ceremony, many city officials have set foot in that park. It seems a gathering place for folks who are down-and-out, drugs and shady deals. The creation of this public park back in 1915 was the only real controversial rebuilding project. The space had been taken by eminent domain. Protestors said that the money should have been spent on schools and public works, not commemoration.

The monument stands in the northwest corner of the park, facing down Washington Street where the fire crossed the tracks, where, today and most days, a man stands in front of a Domino's Pizza in a red and blue Domino's Pizza shirt, holding a huge poster board advertising the special of the day.

The man has stood there, it seems to me, since we moved to Salem over 25 years ago. Back then, he looked like a high schooler. Now, when I bike past him, I see his curly grey sideburns.

*

From the perspective of 100 years, the recovery seems efficient and effective. Power was completely restored to the city by June 27th, two days after the fire, a fact that astonishes when, today, a brutal nor'easter can knock out a neighborhood's power for weeks. The city was rebuilt in the next three years. The factories returned, although the Korn Leather Factory had to move to Peabody. The Naumkeag Steam Cotton Company, which bordered The Point and the Atlantic, and was one of the last buildings to burn, was rebuilt completely by early 1916.

The fire halted Salem's growth, but it was the cheap labor in the south, two decades later, that spelled the end of Salem's industries. After the fire, houses were rebuilt, generally with brick instead of wood. Parks were created with the idea that they might halt the rush of some future fire. New building regulations were established.

Bertram Field's camp emptied out by the second week of July. By mid-August, less than six weeks after the fire, the Forest River Park camp had shut down too. They had housed thousands. Somehow, everyone found a hole to sleep in. And while there was some displacement, there was enough of a community, particularly among the French-Canadians, that most of them remained in the Salem area. The church may have been destroyed, and it wasn't going to be rebuilt in all its glory, but the people survived. They mostly chose to stay, and they mostly were able to do so.

Today, the city's roughly the same size that it was then, nearly 50,000 people; there's tourism, not manufacturing. There are still some French Canadians, some Italians, Irish, Poles, African Americans. And now there are Dominicans, Puerto Ricans, a sprinkling of Vietnamese.

The tanning factories focused on shoes, specifically women's leather shoes, the industry built up in the last decades of the 19th century. Today, they're all gone. A friend tells me about working as a night watchman at the last factory in the early 1980s, after it had been shut down, guarding the abandoned machinery. It was just him and the rats. At the corner of Boston and Essex Street, just up the block from where the fire began, is a new store, Urban Styles, with shrink-wrapped leather sneakers, made in some Asian country. Even the ones on sale cost over $100.

*

Two schools that had burned, Saltonstall and Brown, were combined into one: Saltonstall.

A new fire station was built on Loring Ave. The fire station on Essex was rebuilt.

The Society of Friends Church was rebuilt.

On Endicott Street, just up my block, they cleared an open space.

High Street Park, grimy little park of my children's youth, was created behind the St. Mary's Italian Catholic Church. The church, which, like St. Joseph's, closed during the sex abuse scandal, is now a homeless shelter. The park's still there.

*

In 2017, a year after Donald Trump's election, Salem voted 6756 to 5030 to approve a ballot initiative affirming that Salem would be a sanctuary city, that its police officers and other city officials would not ask about immigration status or seek proof of citizenship from anyone needing service. Tanya Stepasiuk, who chaired the group that advocated for the passage of the ordinance, said, "We need to come together with our neighbors here. We're looking forward to all of Salem coming together. We know people have different views, but we all know we love and care about this city."

Perhaps the reason the fire isn't part of Salem's standard lore is simply because the city recovered, and the scars, like many scars, are smoothed over by new skin. Perhaps the story of the fire is that the recovery went fairly well, that the refugees were sheltered and fed, and that, generally, they found new living conditions in less than two months. That, while the militia was bossy at times, and while those with more groused about those with less getting a little, things proceeded fairly smoothly. The French-Canadian community was big enough and intact enough that it didn't scatter to the wind. Those who left Salem found housing in surrounding towns. I have descendants from those communities in my classes at Salem State today.

Of course, the monuments are almost invisible. What changed doesn't tell us it changed. The fireproof roofs, the brick triple-deckers, Lafayette Park. The one building that would have best commemorated the fire would have been the rebuilt St. Joseph's church, or at least the huge statue of St. Joseph that surveyed the neighborhood in the ghostly remnants of the church for some 30 years after the fire. But that church disappeared a century after the fire itself, and the interred statue of St. Joseph is deep under the new building erected on the site.

I biked to the front of that building, a squat apartment complex some four stories high, with a new small grocery on the first floor, The Daily Table, which offers discounted food to The Point neighborhood. In the brick wall near the apartment entrance is the concrete cornerstone with "2013" carved in it. Just above that, an old fire emergency box number 5122. Its red and white color is a plastic seal—not paint—and it has been peeled off around the bottom.

I suspect it works.

*

As I was shoveling the inch of show that had fallen, finishing up the path to our backyard, I heard some wailing and swearing from the street in front of the house—someone talking to herself. "A crazy drunk," I thought, and felt glad that there was a little distance between us. Not enough, though. A woman's voice called out through the dark, "Excuse me, excuse me?"

"Yes?"

"Could you help me out? Could you do me a favor?"

I walked toward the front. "Well, what is it?"

A woman stood in the street, shivering. She wore a thin coat and looked a bit off balance; it seemed clear that she'd been crying. She needed a ride to the hospital, she said. This had been the worst day of her life. It was her birthday, and her boyfriend had broken up with her, had walked away from her on the street, and when she asked him to slow down, he just kept going. She had shattered a bone in her leg some weeks ago and had taken the cast off because it had started to smell, but now she could hardly walk. And it was her birthday. She was 40.

"Let me tell my wife," I said. I opened the front door, and Eileen heard the story, too. Her voice instantly took on the tender tone she used when a child was hurt. I grabbed my keys, and the woman and I got into our car.

In the car, she kept thanking me. It turned out she didn't want to go to the hospital after all. "I'm not gonna lie to you. I'm not going to the hospital. I'm going to the woods near the school. Next to the hospital I have a friend with a tent. Gonna sleep in a tent."

"You sure you don't want to go to the hospital?" I asked. "That sounds cold."

I drove her the five blocks to the middle school, and she told me a lot about herself, all while thanking me extravagantly. "You're a saint," she kept saying.

She told her story again. She had gone to the shelter. She had gone to the police. Nobody would help. "You can probably tell that I had a few drinks," she said. She was just in a bad spot now. "I'm not from around here. I've saved people's lives. I'm a photographer."

"It feels good in here," she said. "Feel my hand. Feel how cold." I drove up the sloped lot and parked, left the engine running. I reached out and took her hand. It was cold. We shook. I looked more carefully at her. She had a nose ring, dark longish hair, and she wore a pair of oversized sweatpants.

She looked straight at me and said again, “Really, you’re a saint,” then opened the door and eased her leg out. She turned back to thank me one more time, then limped off to cross the basketball court, heading toward the small, wooded hill. I watched her go. I could hardly stand it, seeing her hobble off into the cold dark, barely able to walk. Was there even any shelter for her in those woods, or was that just a hopeful dream?

That hill had once held plenty of tents, shelters for those displaced by the fire. I watched her walk toward it, and I dreamed of rows of ghost tents still standing, and some kind citizens offering food and clothing, making sure she would get through the night.

NOTES

The majority of the information in this essay is drawn from the following sources, as well as from *The Salem Evening News.*

Great Salem Fire 2014, Digital Commons at Salem State University. (SSU)

Arthur B. Jones, *The Salem Fire.* Boston, The Gorham Press. 1914. (SF)

Barbara Pero Kampas, *The Great Salem Fire of 1914: Images From the Phillips Library Collection*. Charleston, SC, The History Press. 2008. (GSF)

Montayne Perry, *The Salem Fire Relief.* Salem, MA, Milo A. Newhall & Co. 1915. (SFR)

Jacob A.C. Remes, *Disaster Citizenship: Survivors, Solidarity, and Power in the Progressive Era.* Chicago, University of Illinois Press. 2016. (DC)

1 "The intersection of Proctor . . . jagged potholes," Since the writing of this essay, Boston Street has been repaved and the area is busy with new construction.

2 "burning 1376 buildings and leaving over 15,000 homeless," GSF, quoting *The Salem Evening News*, June 25, 1915: 59. Other estimates have at least 18,000 homeless (DC).

3 "The Saturday after the fire . . .," GSF says 200-500 thousand estimated to have come in on the Saturday after the fire, citing *The Salem Evening News*, June 28, 1914: 74. Jones, in *The Salem Fire*, writes that "it is said there were one million people in Salem on the night of June 25th," though this most likely refers to relief workers as well as tourists. This seems almost certainly an exaggeration: 105.

4 "It turns out that, yes, the plaque . . . was put up in 1964 . . .," Email conversation with Salem historian, Donna Seger.

5 "Commemoration privileges . . . yields no moral," Dane Anthony Morrison and Nancy Lusignan Schultz, *Salem: Place, Myth, and Memory* (Boston, Northeastern UP. 2004), "Introduction": 6.

6 "brick lies between the inner and outer walls of my house," A recent visit by an insulation company revealed this is probably not true.

7 "homeless slept in the cemetery . . . a child was born there," SSU.

8 "Conflagration" section. The path of the fire which follows is documented in SF (35-44) and GSF (34-58).

9 "Arthur Jones tells a story . . .," SF: 99-100.

10 "a Civil War veteran . . .," SF mentions Withey dying in his house: 43.

11 "Seeing his car on fire," SSU.

12 "Firemen sat in puddles," photo in GSF: 110.

13 "Among the sixty injured . . . flying nozzles," SF: 43.

14 "Militia clearing neighborhoods . . . found three babies," SF: 117.

15 "Three days after the fire . . .," GSF: 16

16 "They worked in 1914 . . . battling the original blaze," These facts about the response to the fire are found in several sources, including SF and GSF.

17 "In a photo . . .," This photo and the others mentioned in this section, as well as the advertisement in the *Boston Globe,* can be found in SSU.

18 "It's at the end of my block . . . next to the senior center," The senior center has been moved to a new location, right near where the fire started, just off Boston Street. The building remains.

19 "Let those whose faith in humanity . . . human race in its entirety," SFR: 76-77.

20 "assumed no responsibility . . .," GSF: 35.

21 "Someone good at figures . . .," SF: 21.

22 "Recalling the fire . . .," Orille L'Heureux's memory is recorded in Elizabeth Blood and Elizabeth Duclos-Orsello's video, *Le Grand Feu: Franco-American Memories of the Fire.*

23 "if the factory had been equipped . . .," SF: 36.

24 "After the fire, Max Korn had to rebuild in Peabody," GSF: 38.

25 "Three French, one Italian, and one American," SF: 116.

26 "Tecla. Gone to Brockton," SF: 117.

27 "*The Salem Evening News* blamed the fire . . .," *The Salem Evening News,* July 2, 2014: 11.

28 "given the name 'Shackles'," SF: 111.

29 "After the fire, the shell of the church . . .," The material on St. Joseph's church and statue is from *The Salem Evening News*' articles "Workers find Statue of St. Joseph in Salem," May 14, 2013 and "Heard Around Town: the Story behind the St. Joseph Statue," May 17, 2013.

30 "an even more beautiful edifice," *The Salem Evening News,* 2 July 1914: 12; qtd. in DC.

31 "the most expensive chocolate in America," from a conversation with Harbor Sweets founder, Ben Strohecker. Strohecker, who passed away in 2016, kept a tag hanging from his car's rear view mirror as a reminder: "DBASH." Don't be a shithead.

32 "The largest and longest standing refugee camp . . .," The following material on the Forest River Camp comes from a number of sources. The material at the beginning of the paragraph is from *Great Salem Fire*: 17. The material at the end of the paragraph, about the refugees personalizing their space and the rituals of the camp, were from DC, Chapter Three: "It Is Easy Enough to Establish Camps: Geographies of Community and Resistance in Burned Salem": 78-104.

33 "The Red Cross . . .," This paragraph, including the list of items, is from GSF: 97-99.

34 "A local band played concerts . . .," DC: 81.

35 "as heard in the sermons at the time . . .," A summary of the Salem churches' responses to the fire is found in DC, in Chapter Six, "The Sufferings of This Time Are Not Worthy to Be Compared with the Glory That Is to Come": 165-75.

36 "The Jews insisted on . . . a kosher cook," DC: 95-96.

37 "although Salem is over three-quarters white . . . majority white to latino," Salem's demographics: https://worldpopulationreview.com/us-cities/massachusetts/salem#demographics

Salem high school demographics: http://profiles.doe.mass.edu/profiles/student.aspx-?orgcode=02580505&orgtypecode=6.

38 "Captain Blanchard . . .," DC: 85-86.

39 "Arthur Tremblay's . . . against liquor laws," DC: 98.

40 "some youngster to pick up rubbish," *The Salem Evening News*, 3 July 1914: 6.

41 "she got past the guards . . .," *The Salem Evening News*, 12 July 1914: 2.

42 "When the smoke hadn't yet cleared . . . I see his curly grey sideburns," Since this essay's composition, Lafayette Park has been spruced up by the city, and it doesn't have the seedy feel it once did. The monument to the fire has been buffed clean and, curiously, moved from one corner of the park to a somewhat more central location. The man with the greying sideburns has not been seen recently.

43 "Power was completely restored . . .," GSF: 69.

44 "Naumkeag Steam Cotton Company . . . rebuilt by 1916," GSF: 174.

45 "The tanning factories focused on shoes . . .," GSF: 22.

46 "Two schools that had burned . . . . The park's still there," This list of changes to the Salem landscape is taken from GSF: 153.

47 "In 2017 . . . care about this city," *The Salem Evening News,* 7 November 2017.

Laid-Off Elementary School Librarian

When the new principal
under the direction
of the educational
consulting company
asks you to train
your minimum-wage replacement
and the local papers
praise all the "reforms"
and even your friends
move to the suburbs and believe
the brown skin of the children you teach
must be avoided,
when your Saturdays
buying used books for those children
and the darkening afternoons
putting those books away
so they can check them out again
seem a lost, wasted life,
remember your walk
to and from school
through the downtown
that's still your downtown
and the way your students
wrap their arms around your leg
when they see you on the street
and how the older ones
from years before—

even, sometimes, the boys—
hug you in Market Basket
or at the Halloween Parade
and pronounce your name
wrong, like they used to,
Mizgerald, Mizgerald!
and then tell you
what books they've been reading.

Winter Island Vow

for E.F.

“Life’s too short not to jump in the ocean every day,”
said an old man one afternoon, scooping the Atlantic
and slapping it across his chest, and so
we have tried to jump in the ocean every day—
well, every day in summer.

It’s only a ten-minute ride from our house—
a small, tame, nearly empty beach
—and we drop our bodies into the brine,
wiggling our limbs in a slow dance.
We talk about her work, mine,
review our children, nearly adults, note
a backlit cloud, some local news,
and gossip, always a dab of gossip.

Above us, the late day sky spreads
pink and rose over the sailboats,
the old arcade, the bridge that spans
the river’s mouth. On the slime-coated rocks,
a young girl and boy clamber for hermit crabs,
collect them in a green pail.
Their mother sits on a towel, gazing past us.

When they shift the pail, I hear the splash and rattle
all the way from here, where we dog paddle,
keeping our promise to ourselves
in the meager waves, out just over our heads.

THE SCHOOL

"In a republic like ours, children must be educated . . . so as to be above pride as well as above abasement."

—Horace and Mary Peabody Mann, from *Life of Horace Mann* by Mary Peabody Mann, 1865.

Breathing

Only in winter, through a tangle of leafless branches, can I see from my office window the two smokestacks of the coal-burning power plant that rise over the city of Salem. Light beige, with soot smearing the upper parts, they seem the tallest structures north of Boston. A white light blinks atop the highest chimney every second or so like a heartbeat. The city's air quality is bad, and the plant is one of the major reasons. It is one of Massachusetts' "filthy five," plants that, because of their age, were exempted from legislation regulating pollution levels.

When I accepted a job to teach at Salem State College, my family and I moved to this city, and both my son Aidan and I developed asthma. That first winter and spring, Aidan, just one year old, had to have a machine—a nebulizer for infants—pump an airy spray of Albuterol four times daily into his lungs, including once in the middle of the night, to ensure that his airways stayed open. At first Aidan resisted, and we, not wanting to aggravate him and exacerbate his breathing problems, simply held the mask near his face, hoping he'd breathe in some of the vapors as they dispersed into our apartment. Eventually, we had to pin him down over his screams. Thankfully, he grew to like the treatment and even found it soothing.

Once, before my asthma had been diagnosed, I let my class out early and had my wife pick me up at the campus to rush me to the doctor. I could hardly breathe. In class, I had been coughing my way through a poem, wheezing at every line break. Granted, it could have been anything that made me suddenly asthmatic at age thirty, but whenever I look at the stained smokestacks, or notice the layer of black grime on cars or windows, I blame the power plant.

My first semester at the college, one of my students told me about an uncle who was a serial killer and buried his victims' bones in his yard. That surprised me, even shocked me—then. I suspected that she was putting me on. Now, having taught here for six years, such information would barely register. "Really?" I might say. "Huh." This past semester, I had five students with bipolar disorder and one who was married to a gay man for fifteen years. One of my best writing students attempted suicide.

There was one part of the serial killer story that was unusual: as my student told me, "they wrote a book about him." A book! The story was more sensational than the unrecorded miseries of many of my students—struggles with abusive boyfriends, poverty, addictions of friends and family members, and, of course, car accidents (it must be a Salem State graduation requirement: car demolition—three credits). It is as if the foul air from the looming power plant, slowly choking our children, has seeped into the students, making their lives—but not their souls—hard and bitter and unhealthy.

If only their suffering weren't so anonymous, and their accomplishments were recognized. Every year, Salem State graduates dozens of students who are parents. A few years ago, an unmarried Harvard student with a child got involved in a custody battle, and *The Boston Globe* ran a series of stories on her. No paper spotlights the unwed parents at Salem State, and they rarely have anyone fighting to take care of their kids. When their children wake up sick and can't go to school, they bring them to my classes, where they can hear a discussion of Langston Hughes' "Little Lyric (of Great Importance)": "I wish the rent / was heaven sent."

How much I owe these students, how much I have learned. They know the score; they know they are losing by a lot before the game even begins, and they shrug, as if to say, "What am I supposed to do, cry?"

Salem State students don't perform as well on standardized tests as Harvard students do. So what? They can tell you where to go—or not to go—to get your car fixed. I ask a student whose stepfather is a mechanic, "Be honest: do they rip you off?"

"Yeah," he replies, "sort of. They just tell you that you should replace lots of things that don't really need replacing. They make you buy things you don't need."

Make you buy things you don't need. Like a diploma from a private university. Make you want to be something you're not. He knew the score. I leave my car unlocked. It's a piece of junk, a thirteen-year-old station wagon that qualifies as a compact car in today's age of SUVs. It's even got an old tape player, and I leave a bunch of tapes—most without cases—in plain view. No one's ever bothered with it.

In class, I pass out a page from a William Carlos Williams lecture on poetry. "I was going to copy the whole essay," I say, "but we can't afford it—budget cuts." I shrug. "Call your congressman."

At a recent meeting with a committee of outside evaluators of the college, a Salem State faculty member described our students as heroic. I knew what she meant. The faces under the cheap, rented mortarboard at graduation are those of heroes. A degree from Salem State means something: it often means one has endured. If, in most circles, it means less than a degree from Harvard, it also should mean more.

But wait. Heroic? Late last semester I walked into my seminar class—the only seminar I've ever taught at the school—and no students were there. Eventually four of the eight found their way, but only one had done any of the reading. Thinking fast, I got a James Baldwin video from the library, and we watched it, watched him saying, "The starting point, the bottom line is, we are all brothers. If you can't take it from there, you can't take it at all," his eyelids flashing, eyes pushing out from their sockets.

Every few months, I come across an article by or about an inspiring teacher (usually of high school English) that reminds me that what I do is valuable and honorable. And yet, the day-to-day realities often overwhelm: the students who disappear, the ones who probably will, all the missed classes. I work with troubled students, and what makes their lives seem even more tragic is that they're smart—smart enough to know they're troubled. You would not believe me if I listed what my students have endured in the last year alone: a mother's botched brain surgery; the death of a sister—a mother of two—and the subsequent alcohol binge of the father; car accidents (several); a sister's overdose; a mother jailed for dealing; bouts with anorexia, depression, drugs . . . . Then there are the "nontraditional" students—adults who have already made it through cancer, divorces, foster-home childhoods, homelessness, madness. Misery upon misery, often endured while working two jobs.

Unavoidably, their struggles seep into my own life. One semester I got several harassing phone calls from—I found out long afterward—a student's jealous ex-boyfriend. I never quite got used to the haunting Police song "Don't Stand So Close to Me" droning through my phone or, when I refused to pick up, playing on my answering machine at 12:30 in the morning.

Out my office window, the drab window shades of Meier Hall stare back at me, some off-white, some curdled cream. Beyond them, Salem State's own smokestack, which three years ago malfunctioned and spewed ash all over the neighborhood, rises out of the administration building. And just past that, the Sullivan Building, over a hundred years old, squats as if it knows something heavy, something true. Or perhaps it's just hunkering down, pressure squeezing the bricks off the facade.

I'm in it for the long haul. Last spring, the letters arrived, first from the college president, then from the board of trustees: tenure. With any luck, I'll get raises and promotions down the line, and my family and I will be able to afford life.

Aidan and I, five years older, are both much better. I take a puff from my inhaler before basketball at the Salem Y; he hardly ever needs one. We've acclimated. Our lungs have come to accept what floats between us, around us. We'll both probably die early because of it, the grit of this world.

I wonder if, in the years to come, I will still get teary at Salem State's graduations. The ceremony is simple, the setting plain. In the hockey arena, traces of sweat from the last season mingle with spring's scents drifting through the open doors. The deans, having practiced, pronounce the names—Tuttle, Corcoran, Brodeur, Carney—almost correctly, though they fail to drop the r's. The ice is long gone, the silly banners draped about, and many of our graduates are absent, too busy to show up, going about their lives amid the sting of the unclean yet human air of this historic city.

A Good School

It's late afternoon, and the car battery dies while my family and I are at Salem Willows, the amusement park-turned-arcade down the road from Salem's power plant. I need to teach an evening class at Salem State, and a long walk stretches ahead of me. An older couple that had driven over the bridge from Beverly for a bag of popcorn (a Willows' specialty) sees my distress and offers to drive me home. It's out of their way, but they do it cheerfully. On the ride, they find out I'm a professor at the college.

"Our niece went there. She loved it," the man tells me. I'm not surprised. Most people I meet in and around Salem speak appreciatively, even enthusiastically, about the college—either they went there, or they attended one of the theater productions, or they took a night class. This couple's niece had initially attended some well-known school and had disliked it. At Salem State she had small classes taught primarily by professors, not graduate students or part-timers. Her professors knew her name. "It's a good school," her aunt says.

A good school. It's a phrase I first heard in high school, when I was deciding where to apply to college. Thanks to good SAT scores, I received invitations from many colleges, most of which I had never heard: Case Western Reserve, Haverford, Bucknell. These, I was told—by my mother and by the savvy students in my Advanced Placement classes—were "good schools." If I wondered how someone who had never visited these schools could declare with certainty that they were "good," my doubts were erased by examining a guide to colleges, which labeled these schools "highly" or "extremely" competitive.

But what was a "good school"? I'm not sure the answer was clear to me as a prospective student, or to the people writing the guides, for that matter. Only one impression was definite: a good school was one that people wanted to be in and where they felt a sense of importance. These schools weren't all the same; some promised personalities. If you attended Oberlin, you could feel that you were more of a free spirit than if you attended Amherst. Most important, though, if you went to a good school, you could take pride in it because it was a place that many people wanted to go to and not so many were accepted. To get accepted meant that you were among the chosen.

The Ivies seemed the most prestigious, and I ended up at Columbia University, drawn by the teeming streets of New York, and fascinated by James Simon Kunen's account of the 1968 student takeover in his *The Strawberry Statement.* Of course, it also was important that Columbia had chosen me.

The distance between Columbia and Salem State at first seems too great to merit a comparison. Columbia is a world-renowned university, with a price to match. Salem State is an affordable public college in a state whose government cares little about public education. The students at Columbia are generally high achievers, graduates of top private and public high schools from accomplished and educated families. Many students at Salem State are first-generation college students from the less-affluent towns north of Boston. Many aspire to be nurses or high school teachers.

At Columbia, as at other good schools, it is presumed that one will get a "good education," another mushy phrase. According to the college guidebooks, a good education can be quantified: number of publications by faculty, number of books in the library. In its annual ranking of colleges, *US. News and World Report* weighs most heavily a school's endowment and the percentage of applicants it rejects. Just a smidgen of thought reveals how superficial and insignificant these numbers are. In my undergraduate education at Columbia, only a handful of professors inspired me. The most influential one I had only by accident, when he replaced a more famous professor who took a midsemester leave of absence after suffering a nervous breakdown. Did I count professors' publications before I enrolled in their classes? Did these publications make a whit of difference to my classroom experience? As an English major, I was one of fifty to a hundred students in the class. No one knew, or seemed to know, whether I showed up.

At some prestigious schools, most undergraduates rarely get into classes with the prestigious faculty, and are taught instead by graduate students or adjuncts, part-timers who often shuttle among three or more campuses, collecting a pittance for their labor. Last summer, I had brunch with some faculty at Red's Diner, another Salem institution. Our waitress mentioned that she was thinking of going back to school and was considering Salem State. We got to talking. She had gone to Boston University for a year and hated it. Now in her mid-twenties, she had recently returned from traveling and working in South America, and she had been taking courses at a community college. "And you know what?" she said, "I took two classes with the same teachers I had at B.U. And I was paying how much at B.U.?"

Mainly, a "good education" seems to mean that a diploma from the school makes you eligible for a "good job." *A good job.* A former student shares a bit of wisdom: in Los Angeles, everyone asks where you're from; in New York, everyone asks what you do; and around Boston, even if you're middle-aged, everyone asks what college you attended. When I think about how these attitudes affect my students, part of me is infuriated at the injustice. Yet another part of me thinks it is just as well. Why have our students strive to join that "good" world? If people are superficial enough to believe that money buys a better education, we want nothing to do with them anyway, do we? For the people I meet, like the older couple who gave me a lift, Salem State is a "good school." Is that enough?

What is the difference between Salem State and Columbia? At Salem State, accessible professors teach many of the students' courses, the classes are generally smaller than those at Columbia, and students aren't conferred a sense of entitlement upon graduation. Of course, there are also the other students: at a school like Columbia, which is devoted to accepting high achievers, one's classmates can be inspiring. It's not so easy to develop lifelong bonds at Salem State, where fellow students often rush to their cars after class to get to work or pick up their kids. I wish I could grant them the leisure to live the contemplative life that Columbia offers. Yet being among Salem State students, who often scramble to pay for school and try, not always successfully, to squeeze in the time to go to classes, can be eye-opening and inspiring as well. During the latest war in Iraq, I asked a class–"How many of you have a friend or relative over there?" Eighteen out of twenty students raised their hands. I wonder what the numbers would be in a Columbia classroom.

I meet Tony on the back elevator in the library. He's in his mid-thirties, wearing the blue striped shirt of the maintenance workers, "Anthony" scripted in a white oval on the breast. We exchange hi's.

"You teach here, right?" he asks.

"Yeah, English."

"I took all my English classes," he says. "I'm a history major. I want to teach high school, go back and work with all those teachers I gave a hard time." He smiles.

"Good luck," I say.

When I get off the elevator, I'm still thinking about Tony. It isn't that he is so unusual—a full-time maintenance worker who is also a full-time student; it is that he is, it seems, so wonderfully typical here. The same person who is keeping the buildings up is taking classes in them. The gap between the blue-collar employees and students is so much smaller at Salem State than at all those schools I desired to attend. In this case, the employee and student were one and the same. And, better yet, he wanted to return to his community, to become a teacher.

What is there to say? I work at a good school.

It Grows Back: Three Students

Some years ago, I wrote an essay about Salem State, the university where I have taught for over a decade, suggesting that students get just as good an education, albeit a different one, than students at more prestigious universities. The article went viral, and I got several emails, including one from a man in Oregon who suggested that if college was all about status, not learning, why go to college? Why not step away from the rat race and forge one's own life and education?

It's a romantic notion. It might work for a few people, but given what I have seen in my time at Salem State, it's hard to say that higher education is not improving students' lives. I am not speaking about the job opportunities that it ends up offering, either, but the opening of the eyes and mind that happens, at least a little bit, to even the most uninspired college student.

I have audited several dance classes at Salem State. In one of those classes, there was a tall young man who seemed out of place. He was the only other male in the class, and he looked like one of those guys who hung out in the gym playing pick-up basketball. This would be a tough class for him, some sort of requirement.

This story doesn't have a surprise ending—he didn't pass with flying colors and impress everyone with his final performance. He only lasted half the semester. I never learned his name, and I don't know if he even stayed in school. He wasn't a particularly good dancer, though he did try to learn the steps. I seem to remember him wincing through the stretches (or was that just me?).

So, was this simply a failure? A man came to class and tried something he had never tried before. He got better at it, and he learned a little about his body, about form, about focus. I got a kick watching him in the mirror trying to hold a leg up, or skipping and spinning across the glossy wooden floor. I am certain that he learned something.

Tina

It isn't just that students like the one above take something intangible from a class, but that I, and the other students, take something valuable from them. Teaching at Salem State, I hear a lot of stories: the mother who lost her husband early and was trying to stay enrolled, but at last couldn't afford it; the woman who lived in a shelter with her infant; the man who had grown up in the projects. At thirty-six, he had suffered a serious motorcycle accident, then decided to come to college. "I just wish I had done this a lot earlier," he said to me.

For years I've believed that my students bring a certain wisdom to the class, a wisdom that doesn't score on the SAT or other standardized tests. The old teaching cliché—I learn from my students—feels true, but it is hard to explain. I'm not particularly naïve. I know that life can be difficult. So it is not that my students initiate me into the world of sorrow. It is that they often bring their sorrows, and their struggles, to the material, and when they do, it makes life and literature seem so entwined as to be inseparable. Like Tina.

Tina, an African American student from a rough neighborhood, was one of the students in the class who read the books. She loved certain characters: Zora Neale Hurston's fun-loving Tea Cake and Toni Morrison's defiant, mysterious Sula; I remember, too, that she was torn between Martin Luther King, Jr. and Malcolm X. She even visited me in my office once or twice to seek advice about problems with a roommate or a professor.

Once, late in the semester, Tina came to my office because she had missed class and wanted to turn in her paper. My African American literature class had just finished Richard Wright's novel, *Native Son.* It is a brutal book, whose protagonist, a poor young black man, Bigger Thomas, murders two women, and shows very little regret. Readers, to this day, are not sure what to make of Bigger. Is he to be pitied? Is he a warning? A symbol? A product of American racism? Is he too much a stereotype?

The class had read essays by African American writers James Baldwin and David Bradley criticizing *Native Son* and had been asked to evaluate them. Baldwin, Tina tells me, was hard, "but he was such a good writer." Did she agree with Baldwin, I ask. Was Bigger denied humanity by Wright? How does she feel toward him?

"I think he needs help," she says, "but I felt sorry for him. I wanted him to be able to understand his life—" I cut in, offering some teacherish observation about how Bigger shows glimmers of understanding in the last part of the book, but her mind is far ahead of me, just waiting for me to stop. I do.

"The book reminded me of the guy who killed my uncle. You probably saw it—the trial was all over the TV last week." I shake my head.

The man and an accomplice had murdered her uncle, a Dorchester storeowner, three years ago, and the previous week had been sentenced to life without parole. The two had been friends of the uncle's family, had played pool with the uncle the night before, planning to rob and kill him the next day.

"When I saw him sitting there, with his head down, looking all sad, I don't know, I felt sorry for him. I wanted to give him a copy of *Native Son*. I wanted to walk up to him and put it in his lap. It might help him to understand his life."

She looks at me, her light brown face just a few shades darker than mine. She's nineteen. Her hair is pinned back, but some strands float loose. Her eyes are wide as half dollars, as if she's asking me something. Without thinking, I nod slowly, trying to hold her gaze. On the shelves surrounding us are the papers and books of my profession, that giant horde of words that will pursue me until I die.

"My family wants him to suffer—hard. But I want to talk to him. Do you think that's bad? I want to know why he did it, what happened. I wonder how he'd react if he saw me—what he'd do if I gave him the book."

I imagined *Native Son* in the man's lap. The glossy purple, green, and black cover bright against the courtroom's muted wood, the man's trousers. His hand, smooth with youth, holds its spine. His thumb blots out part of the eerie full-lipped face on the front. As the words of the court fall about him, the book rises and falls ever so slightly, as if breathing.

When I wrote the first draft of that scene, I was still in the middle of teaching that African American literature class. It struck me then, and it still strikes me now, as a strong argument for the value of what happens in college. Although one colleague found Tina's wish to give the book to the young man absurd (I remember her laughing when I read it aloud), to me the episode spoke of the way a book and the class dialogue about it can allow one to re-envision a life, or the world. Although Tina probably never gave him the book, the fact that she desired to do so, and that her desire triggered in my head the image of the man holding the book in the courtroom, seems important. Student and teacher both develop empathy, imagination, and maybe even a little wisdom. Can we ask much more from our work as educators?

By the time I wrote the final draft of the essay, the semester was over, and there was some new information that I considered including, but eventually cut. Tina, good student though she was, had not finished the semester. Personal and financial difficulties led her to leave school, and she never did make up the incomplete that I gave her. I saw her once on campus that summer—"Hey, Scrimgeour," she called out to me as I was playing tennis with my sons. She told me that she had plans to return to a college nearer her family eventually. Life being what it is, I had my doubts she would ever get a degree.

Though I didn't include these details about Tina's future in the original essay, they seemed important to me later, rising up from the past to challenge my assumptions about the value of the moment the essay describes. What did that moment mean? It didn't get her through that semester, that class. It may not have changed her relationship with her uncle's killer, and if it did, it may not have changed it for the better. Who is to say that Tina even remembers that conversation now? I did give her a copy of the essay, but these things get lost, misplaced, recycled, tossed.

In a sense, the moment seemed too easy a triumph. And too small: a speck of water in a desert, evaporating before this sentence is finished, nothing substantial enough to be nourishing. Given that I didn't know whether Tina would ever finish college, whether she would ever find rewarding employment, or happiness, how much value can I really ascribe to that conversation in my office? Sure, for me it was moving (and I got an essay out of it!), but what about for her? Was I deluding myself? Should I insist on something different, or something more, from teaching?

Maybe it's not about her, or about me. Maybe it's about the words I wrote, the words I write, the act of making something of the details of our lives. The world moves so quickly and arbitrarily, but the scene on the paper remains, illuminating something, not necessarily for Tina, or for me, but for some anonymous reader, a young teacher, maybe, who wonders about the value of what she does, wonders whether, in the flood of incompletes we live with, it's worth it to keep teaching.

LaTeisha

Tina ended up in my class because of a recommendation from a friend of hers, LaTeisha, a student who had been in a previous African American literature class. For the first month of that class, LaTeisha was one of my most frustrating students. It wasn't because of anything that she said. She rarely spoke. But she spent most of the class with a pout on her dark brown face. She seemed to talk with the other students before and after class, and so I began to blame her surliness for the class's general malaise. I wondered if she was one of those African American students who resented a white professor teaching African American literature.

Things began to change when she came up after class to ask me something about Frederick Douglass. I don't recall the question now, but it was a smart one, and suddenly I knew that she had been paying attention. Soon, she was talking in class. She was especially good at asking simple, real questions. Once, I had laid out a set of ways to think about a book, and she raised her hand and asked, "What do you think?" I still love that: how she recognized that I didn't have the only answer, and also how she honestly was curious what I thought.

Salem State has a program, "Take Your Professor to Lunch," in which students are encouraged to go to lunch with a professor on the university's dime. The hope is that by bringing students and faculty together informally, students will feel more connected to the university and academics. It will help them stay in school and get more out of it. Hardly anyone took advantage of this program, but I did. I would announce it in my classes and wave my datebook around. Every semester at least two or three students would take me up on it. LaTeisha was always one of those students.

At those lunches, I began to learn more about her. When she was seven, LaTeisha and her three sisters—all whose names began with "La" (LaToya, etc.)—had been removed from their house because their mother was addicted to drugs. She was eventually adopted and moved from California to Lowell, Massachusetts, where she attended Lowell High School. She was religious. Once, when it came up that I was an atheist and had been raised in a non-religious household, she said, "I can't imagine what that would be like." She had gotten into Salem State through a special program designed for students who didn't necessarily have the test scores to be admitted unreservedly. I discovered, too, that the pout that had so irked me was simply the face she made when she was thinking hard. We laughed about that, and I discovered, too, that she had a brilliant smile.

LaTeisha came to mind when I collaborated with Caitlin Corbett, a professor of dance, on a semester-long teaching project. We wanted to get a group of students who would combine memoir and movement into an interdisciplinary piece. We didn't necessarily want all the students to have experience in both writing and dance. LaTeisha had experience in neither. I asked her to be part of it anyway. It was asking a lot of a criminal justice major with almost no artistic experience, someone who had gotten into Salem State through a special program, but LaTeisha tried it.

The project was very challenging for Caitlin and me, and also for the seven students. We had a hard time motivating them; it was tough simply getting them to show up to our weekly meetings. Somehow, though, they took charge of the piece, and the final product, which they performed in front of an audience of some 50 students and faculty, was curious and curiously moving: snippets of words about all of their lives recited along with movements—together and apart. For the piece, LaTeisha wrote a little about her forehead:

> *It begins shortly after my hairline and ends right above my eyebrows. It is bigger than most. That used to be a bad thing. I used to hate it and hide it from the kids at school who couldn't appreciate its uniqueness.*
>
> *We feel connected because we've been through a lot together. Today, she goes where I go. Usually she gets there first, and lets me know what's going on. She's a star, and she likes to shine. She is a gift from my father, the sole identifier of the LaLa girls, my sisters.*

I have not asked LaTeisha about it, but I bet she remembers those words. She had to memorize them, and this is what she wrote about being in the production afterwards:

> *I learned that I had grown into my skin. Being able to read the piece about my forehead aloud gave me confidence in a body part I used to feel so insecure about. I have recited my writing to a few friends who could not attend the performance, and their reactions have been, "You actually read that out loud?" I say "Yup," and then we laugh together.*

LaTeisha finished up her degree and graduated, and that summer I saw her around campus. She was working at Salem State, in the testing services area, scheduling student competency tests. As a senior, she had applied to Suffolk Law School, but she didn't get in. "That's too bad," I said, "but you can always try again."

When I ran into her that summer, I proposed that we meet every week or so during the fall, just to check in. "I'd like to do that," she said, so we did. In our early conversations, we discussed her career plans, especially the idea of going to law school or taking some courses to get a job as a paralegal. She really didn't know what she wanted to do, though, and I could tell that the idea of law school intimidated her.

I tried to convince her not to write off law school. Too many Salem State students don't believe they're good enough, and I had confidence in LaTeisha. I had seen her think about issues in my literature classes, I had seen her participation in that semester-long project.

Still, getting into law school would be a challenge. I thought that she wrote well enough and was sharp enough that once she was in, she'd get by, but she had to put in the work to get in, and if she wasn't that interested, she'd have a hard time putting in the work. When we would meet, she would tell me about new ideas she had—a friend of hers had mentioned hairdressing, or modeling, or . . . . Meanwhile, we started studying for the LSAT. Each week we'd both try some problems on our own, then discuss them together. As someone for whom the math and logic questions come fairly easy, I found this a fun challenge. LaTeisha didn't, but she was game, and she'd get some questions right. She was quite good with the reading comprehension. She could follow the drift of an idea well, had a feel for the significance of a transition. We planned, tentatively, that she would take an LSAT prep course in the spring.

As the semester wore on, though, she seemed to lose focus, and toward the end of it, she said that she wasn't really that interested in law school, that she wondered if maybe other people were more interested in her going to law school than she was. "I understand completely," I said, shrugging. "Just don't do it."

She was looking down, and now she lifted her head and faced me. "I want to tell you something," she said, "It's something I haven't told anyone."

Although I tried not to show it, inwardly I cringed. What problem had come up? I thought of all the things that derail my students' dreams—pregnancies, abusive boyfriends, the sudden loss of a job. What was it? Would she be able to handle it? I could tell that, whatever it was, it was important to her, something that had been gnawing at her. What?

I looked right back at her. "Sure, you can tell me. What is it?"

"I didn't apply to law school," she said. "Back when I was a senior, people kept asking me, so I said that I had."

At that moment, I was only relieved. I had feared something else, and so I brushed off this confession. It wasn't a big deal, I told her, and I believed that. Looking back, though, I see that it was a big deal for her. She had lied to her teachers, mentors, and peers. She had created an image of herself as someone who played by the rules and lost, when in fact, she hadn't entered the game.

LaTeisha's decision not to apply was surprisingly familiar. Every year, on national surveys, our students rank notably low on self-confidence, much lower than their actual abilities should merit. In a state with a strong private school network, public education is the poor stepsister, a fact that our students have internalized. Too often, our students assume that they aren't good enough; the state tells them they don't deserve decent funding; the best graduate schools won't even consider their applications. LaTeisha's confession made me want to tell her—*See, you can do it. You just need to apply!*

But she wasn't telling me because she needed someone to nudge her back onto the track toward law school. She had considered law school, had checked out the LSAT, and she had decided no. Perhaps our meetings all year weren't about getting her into law school, but about her getting to that point where she could be honest about herself with another person, where she could share a secret. There are many kinds of success.

In the depths of my computer, I have one other LaTeisha line from that memoir and movement project. We had asked students to make a list of places they had been. Here's what LaTeisha recited:

> *I've been to a pond, the "church," North Carolina, and downtown Salem on Halloween.*

That's a good start, I think—a good start to a good life.

Kol

"I'm thinking of buying a house," Kol tells me, her shy smile framed by her straight black hair. "I've been approved for $300,000." I'm stunned. That's more than I could be approved for on my professor's salary, a modest $64,000.

She's standing in the doorway to my office. She just stopped by to say hello, was too busy to sit in the chair I cleared off for her.

"Wow. You must be making good money."

"I made 70,000 dollars last year. I work three jobs. I'm working eighty hours a week."

Kol, like LaTeisha, had been in my African American literature classes a few years ago. She was a good student. She understood that I wanted to hear and read her opinions, and her participation and papers reflected that understanding. Her writing was workmanlike, and she missed a few classes, but she tried to do the reading, and she was generally engaged—I remember how, in a discussion of slavery, she seemed especially aware of how it severed families. The second semester that I had her, she missed more classes. Her brother was having mysterious medical problems, fainting and vertigo, and she said she was busy trying to get him help. "We don't have insurance," she told me, "and we don't know what's wrong." When she did come to class, her head often drooped to the desktop.

That year, she wasn't working nearly so much as she is now. She lived in the dorms and received financial aid. Until her brother got sick, she seemed to be enjoying herself, enjoying school. Now, Kol, 22, works at the hospital, the mall, and at a doctor's office. Eighty hours. At the doctor's office, she works as a translator for Thai-Americans. "Nobody was coming to the office when I was away," she tells me.

She was away for a month this summer. "I went to Thailand," she says in a voice that suggests she is still amazed at the fact. It had been her first time there. "I went with my family. I wasn't born there. I was born in Cambodia . . . because of the war."

She tells me how different it is, how they use car batteries for electricity and have to charge them daily. How the adults are gone all day, working, leaving the kids alone.

"I have 200 cousins over there. They treated me like a princess. I didn't like that. The little ones would follow me around. They would always try to hold my hand.

"They called me 'stupid' because I didn't know how to wash my own clothes. All the kids there, they're much smarter than they are in America. The two- and three-year olds can do all this work, wash the clothes, wash the dishes."

Since Kol makes so much now, she's not eligible for financial aid. "I try to tell them I'm on my own. I don't get any help from my family, but I have to report their income."

After the semester her brother was sick, Kol moved back into the house her family rented to save money. But that was too crowded. Her sister was sleeping on a sofa in the basement, so Kol gave up her room and moved into a house with four guys, "all partiers." It's hard for her to do her schoolwork there. It would be better, she tells me, if she had her own house. "My family could move in with me." Of the two houses she was looking at, one "needed a lot of work," and one was in a neighborhood with "a lot of gangs."

School isn't what it was when her perky comments brightened my class; it's something to get through as efficiently as possible: "I talk in class to stay awake," she says.

The swarm of contradictions. She makes more than I do, yet lives in a crummy place. She took a month vacation this summer, to Thailand, but she's working eighty hours a week. She's thinking of buying her own house, has been adult enough to live on her own and support herself, yet she's called "stupid" by three-year-old Thai children because she doesn't know how to wash her own clothes without a washing machine. She's curious and motivated, yet college has become a chore for her, more drudgery.

Her life, like many of my students' lives, resists classification: working class, middle-class, bilingual, non-traditional student, oppressed, exploited, success story, first-time homebuyer, second-generation immigrant, first-generation college student, Gen Y, $50,001-$100,000?

Kol doesn't have health insurance. As a student, she can buy it through the college, but, she tells me, it doesn't cover anything. It's not worth $160 a month. And her health is precarious, always has been. Born in a refugee camp, she was not supposed to live. The camp doctor told her mother, who was so malnourished that her skin was becoming transparent, that her daughter had no chance to survive. This difficult beginning may be responsible for Kol's many health problems. In my class, she didn't miss too often, but she has endured ailments, bizarre and mundane, that have regularly filled her life with pain. When I mentioned Kol to a faculty member that works with ESL and international students, she confirmed Kol's medical problems, and she mentioned something else: Kol has visions.

When she comes to see me a few weeks later, on her right wrist—the hand she writes with—she has a wrap, like the one our department secretary wears when her carpal tunnel flares up. She tells me that she has developed a very painful cyst. "I was crying when I was taking my exam," she said. "I need an operation to have it drained, but it costs 5,000 dollars." She knows its cost because she has already had the operation three times. "They tell me there's a 50% chance it will come back," she says. And it has come back, and come back again. She has spent $15,000 removing this cyst; so she can continue school, so she can go to work, so she can write, so she won't be in pain.

The reason she is resisting the operation now isn't that it costs $5,000, but that it costs much more. Having the operation and getting a cast would mean not working for six weeks, and it would make school very difficult. "I can't miss that time," she says.

How valuable is she? How much is her life worth? She wants to go into international business.

I think of the traders on Wall Street, pushing money around to get more money, of the educational bureaucrats dictating what we must teach, what we will be tested on; I think of all those minds that are certain they are winning, that they know more than others. I hold their lives in my palm and examine them—their brittle glitter, the way they insist on their own importance. And then I imagine Kol's life in my other palm: too much work, too many worries. Her life is a muscle—is it the heart?—taut and sinewy and sore.

The cyst. It grows back. You can have it removed, usually at your own expense. You can have it removed four, five, ten times. Fifty percent of the time, it grows back. And it makes you wonder, even though you want to cry it hurts so bad, even though you can barely write through the pain, whether to pay that money to have it removed again because then you're out 5,000 bucks, and you lose your jobs—all three of them—you fail your classes, and, for six weeks at least, even though the pain is gone, you won't be able to write at all.

Fifty percent of the time, it grows back.

Kol says goodbye. Her friend is waiting at the elevator. She's off to class. I lean back in my chair and take a deep breath, then bring my hands together, my fingers locking. My palms don't quite touch, and in the hidden sheaf of air between them, I sense a ghostly heat.

The Swans of Charter Street

The Parlor

. . . this primitive town.
—Mary Peabody, writing about Salem

On top of a bookshelf in the small library of my sons' elementary school in Salem is a bust of Horace Mann, the nineteenth-century educator and reformer often referred to as the father of public education in the United States. The school, like many American public schools, is named after Mann, but he had been dead thirty-seven years when it was founded as a training school for the Salem Normal School. The school changed its name in 1937 as a way to celebrate the centennial of Mann's appointment as the Commonwealth's first secretary of education in Massachusetts, an appointment that marked the beginning of the public education system in the United States.

In 1837, after being appointed secretary, Mann thrust himself into his work with messianic zeal. In his position, he wrote controversial annual reports that shaped the way the Commonwealth and nation came to view public education. These widely read reports were persuasive in part because of Mann's fervor and skilled rhetoric. He writes of one crumbling schoolhouse, "already aware of the danger, the mice have forsaken it." The reports were also persuasive because of the dedication of their author. Mann visited school after school in an effort to determine the state of education and the best course for it to take. He was thorough.

He was vilified by those who did not like his progressive approach—he wanted to fund education with taxpayer money, and he wanted all students, regardless of class, to experience the best education, together, in public schools. This education, Mann felt, must be based on sustaining a child's natural delight in learning and the pleasures of knowledge. It discouraged corporal punishment and encouraged exploration, the development of the whole person. He mentions a Philadelphia businessman who saw students only as future employees and wished that they know simply "how to count to 100 and row a boat to New Orleans." "If others had not known vastly more than this," Mann writes, "there would have been no dollars to count, nor New Orleans to go to" (Mann's words have an eerie echo after the devastation of Hurricane Katrina).

The bust was a gift to the elementary school from the Normal School class of 1937. From a distance, it is elegant and does justice to the handsome Mann. Looking at it, one wouldn't know of Mann's prematurely white hair, which turned when he was 36 after the early death of his first wife. Shoulders back, neck straight, he stares directly into the sunlit room, lips tipped into a faint smile, confidence and wisdom emanating from him.

The bust is yellowed, like coffee-stained teeth. If you tap it, you find that it is not marble but metal. The tinny echo reveals it to be hollow. Across the base, the name "HORACE MANN" was carved inexactly by a long-ago college student, as if with a putty knife. It provides an odd contrast to the finely sculpted face, marking the artistry with a touch of the human.

A few weeks ago my younger son, Guthrie, a kindergartener, reported that kids were claiming there was a ghost in the boys' bathroom.

"A ghost?" I asked. "Are you scared?"

"No. I don't think it's true."

The ghost, the school librarian tells me some days later, was Horace Mann. Some children had come to this conclusion, and it had led to a run on the books the library had about Mann. She laughs. "One student came up and asked me, 'Did he die here?'"

Mann died a long way from here, in Yellow Springs, Ohio, but he did know Salem. He walked its streets, praised its schools, and courted his second wife, Mary Peabody, at her family home at 53 Charter Street, a house that still stands in the heart of this scarred city. He wasn't the only famous person to marry into the Peabody family. Mary's younger sister, Sophia, was courted by Nathaniel Hawthorne in the same house. And it was in this house that the eldest sister, the important intellectual, reformer, and educator, Elizabeth Peabody, first met Hawthorne and helped launch his ascent to literary fame.

The house's illustrious past is obscured by the present. On the outside, at least, it is in disrepair. Painted a drab gray streaked with greenish-black mold, it seems smaller than my family's modest box on Winthrop Street, and, somehow, uglier. It looks as if a semi rumbling down Charter Street could make it collapse, but it has been standing for well over 150 years. If it was larger, more majestic, one could say that it loomed over the ancient Charter Street burying ground beside it, but its three stories seem small, dwarfed by the new glitzy arches of the Peabody Essex Museum across the street. Just a year ago, the museum brought, piece by piece from China, Yin Yu Tang, an eighteenth-century merchant's house, and reconstructed it. The Peabody house faces the back of the Yin Yu Tang, two hundred years of East and West separated by a one-lane street. Though the Chinese house is its nearest neighbor, the Peabody house seems more fastened to the adjacent graveyard, squatting like a large gray monument anchoring the western corner of the grounds. The Salem Witch Memorial, a small rectangular walkway with hewn rock benches carved with the names of each of those put to death in 1692, anchors the eastern side. The graveyard holds the dust of notable early figures, such as John Winthrop, the first governor of the colonies, and Hawthorne's great-great-grandfather, Colonel John Hathorne, Esquire, one of the judges of the witch trials.

When my family moved to Salem, we rented a house on a street named after the judge—Hathorne Street—a block from where I live now. Salem was more affordable than many of the surrounding communities. Unlike its whiter, more affluent neighbors, it was gritty. When I arrived to interview for the position at Salem State, the shuttle driver who took me to my hotel from the airport told me how the city "had been really depressed. It's coming back a little now."

We took to it right away, even though its polluted air helped trigger asthma in our year-old son, Aidan, and me. We walked the Common, we used our Salem residency to get into the Peabody Essex for free, we took Aidan to story hour at the library. When he was healthy enough, we'd take him to nearby High Street Park, the tiny grassless park littered with glass and dog droppings behind St. Mary's Italian Catholic Church, and help him down the slides.

That first fall I would often walk the mile from our house to campus. When I would cross the bridge over the commuter rail tracks, I would occasionally see in the swampy pond off to the left two swans, their whiteness as bright as fire against the murky reflective water. The encroaching houses, and even the roar of a train to and from Boston every half hour, did not scare them away. They seemed a good omen, a small mark of beauty on this place that seemed like it could become my home.

This place, Salem, is old. The city is 150 years older than the United States. Most houses that have historical plaques on them are over 150 years old ("Built for Joseph Cox, Merchant, c. 1810"). On that walk to the college, I pass a house on Jefferson Avenue with an unofficial plaque, hand-painted letters reading "Built by Horace + Henry Michaud 1946." Salem residents would get the joke.

In the unkempt graveyard at the end of my block are the bodies of people who lived three hundred years ago. Many of their names are unreadable now, worn off the old stones. Many of the stones themselves have sunk into the ground, almost buried by three centuries of dirt. Some have fractured and broken; unconnected letters and letter fragments lie about. The town is so heavy with history that no one seems concerned about the loss of a few names every decade or so.

I take my sons to the graveyard in the winter to sled down its faint hills. There needs to be enough snow so that you don't feel the bump of the small stone protrusions, little aches of past, on the way down. For an adult, there needs to be a lot of snow.

If you squeeze through where one of the bars is missing from the graveyard's black iron fence, you will be in the parking lot of the local senior center. The building used to be an elementary school. Beside it is another brick building, the original site of Salem State when it was founded in 1854 as one of Horace Mann's normal schools for teachers. Angle through the lot, cross the street, and head down Cambridge Street, where the modestly well-off live in their tiny antique houses. One block and you reach a vestige of aristocratic Salem, Chestnut Street, broad and tree lined, with grand brick mansions of architectural splendor; it has been called the most beautiful street in America. Its houses, built some two hundred years ago with Salem's great wealth from its shipping industry, routinely sell for well over half a million dollars. It is still the street for Salem's elite, though now they aren't ship captains but lawyers (Horace Mann's first profession), financial advisors, and literary agents.

The distance between Chestnut Street and my family's modest house is far more than the two physical blocks. It is the distance that moved Mann to revolutionize public education, to challenge the ignorance that class prejudice fosters. And the cruelties of this distance, the abuse of power and privilege in his own ancestors, is why the city haunted its native son, Hawthorne.

Born here on July 4, 1804, Nathaniel Hawthorne grew up secluded and doted on by his family, and dreamed of becoming a poet. He lived the majority of his life in the city, though he seemed to dislike it. The aristocratic Salem clashed with Hawthorne's democratic tastes; he "preferred gin to champagne," recalled an acquaintance. Yet, as he explains in "The Custom House," Hawthorne's autobiographical introduction to *The Scarlet Letter*, he is drawn to Salem. His attachment comes from two centuries of ancestors who lived and died here, whose flesh has turned to the dust that spots his shoes as he walks the city's streets. Hawthorne says this attraction is the "mere sensuous sympathy of dust for dust." He will be dead someday, and Salem seems to invite that death. He acknowledges that there is a sentiment within him—"not love, but instinct"—to live in the Salem of his forefathers, yet it is this sentiment that convinced him to leave. "My children have had other birthplaces," he writes—and one hears his sigh of relief—"and, so far as their fortunes may be within my control, shall strike their roots into unaccustomed earth."

Like Hawthorne, I had ancestors here in 1692. Their history has been recorded by my father, himself a poet and teacher. As he followed the tourists' red line painted on the sidewalk past shops full of occult and pagan trinkets and curios, my father, moved by our ancestors' spirits, composed a long poem that blended then and now. One of my ancestors, Mary Towne Eastey, was found guilty of being a witch and was hanged. Another, Thomas Perkins, served on the jury that sentenced her. The persecuted, the judging. The victim, and the one too ignorant or timid to resist lies. There are no accusers in my line, no unrepentant judges. Hawthorne's guilt is not mine. My second son was born in Salem Hospital; his roots have been struck in Salem's dust.

Yet the city haunts me, too. It is hard to reconcile Salem's past with its modest, worn present. There is no narrative that binds the hangings of 1692 to today. The city does not cohere. Hawthorne's essay, "Main Street," which Elizabeth Peabody published in a journal she founded, shows how ungraspable the city was, even in his time. In it, a showman presents a rather two-dimensional pageant of Salem's past while being heckled by an audience member who finds the show obviously phony and simplistic. In the end, the props tumble, and the pageant never gets completed.

The red line on the pavement can't go everywhere, can't tie it all together in an epic loop. It leads tourists from one historic site to the next. It passes the Peabody House but does not point to it. It does not go close to Gallows Hill. The aristocrats, save those on Chestnut Street, have fled. Salem State College, the center of my city, serves the harried working class. The red line is a good long mile away from its industrial brick.

For me, the voices from Salem's past are too numerous, too loud. It is an old city, and the voices merge, cacophonous, with the voices of Salem today—my children and their classmates on the slab of asphalt behind their school, my own struggling students, their writing full of rough music. My father was drawn to our blood ancestors, but I'm drawn to those who do what I do: Horace Mann, the educator, and Hawthorne, the writer. So I step into the nineteenth century, into the house on 53 Charter Street, and sit with Elizabeth, Mary, and Sophia Peabody, with Mann, and with Hawthorne. The babble, for a time, diffuses. They are sturdier than I, and smarter. I'm glad that Sophia, despite her frailty, has come down from her room to join us. It must be the presence of the pensive Hawthorne (my wife can't get over how handsome he is). A talented artist, Sophia draws in the sketchbook on her lap while we converse. I wish she would ask to sketch me, though I'm a bit afraid of what her eye might reveal.

Mary, the middle sister, is the family beauty, but in a social circle that doesn't particularly value looks, she's less of a force than her older sister, Elizabeth, with her powerful intellect, or Sophia, with her seductive sensitivities. Mary has a cleverness with words, though she uses them less often than Elizabeth. Her comments bring appreciative smiles from Mann, which only she—and perhaps Hawthorne—sees. She's more practical and socially conscious than Sophia. When the two younger sisters went to Cuba for a year so that the invalid Sophia might convalesce, Mary was appalled at the slavery she witnessed. Sophia sketched and flirted with the men.

Headstrong Elizabeth has an almost superhuman energy. She is, by all accounts, an inspirational teacher, though it has been said that she lacks a system and is not enough of a drillmaster. Her hair does not stay tucked, but she does not notice, though the others do. She speaks and listens with a fervor that is energizing and a bit terrifying. She has been talking with some of the transcendentalists, especially Mr. Emerson, and, as usual, is bursting with ideas.

Have I been invited?

Even though the conversation is about education, it is lively. A year ago, Mann abandoned a promising law practice and political career to become the Commonwealth's first secretary of education, the first such post in the nation. Almost every friend thought him foolish to take such a low-paying job ($1,500 a year, no expenses) with such little prestige. He has just found out that, after debate, the legislature in Boston voted to renew his fixed contract. "Well, one thing is certain: if I live, and have health, I will be revenged on them; I will do more than 1,500 dollars' worth of good," he says, and smiles, his white hair aglow in the lamplight. He wants to restore the old custom of educating the rich and poor together, and, to that end, wants public schools as good as schools can be made. He despairs at the public's lack of interest in his idea. He will speak on it tonight at the Lyceum in Salem and hopes that more than a handful will turn out.

Elizabeth, who has helped Bronson Alcott run the infamous Temple School in Boston and has published important works about progressive education, encourages him. She's working on her own ideas about education, ones she will eventually put into a scandalous essay, "The Dorian Measure." She will write that public education deserves great sums of money. "It is plain," she'll say, "that if we can spend a hundred million dollars a year for so questionable a purpose as the late war with Mexico, we have resources on which we might draw for public education." And schools should educate the whole self, the spirit of education should be "purely human"; though the common wisdom finds it absurd, she wants to teach gymnastics, dance, music, and art to public school students.

Hawthorne listens, unconvinced. Although he graduated from Bowdoin College, his education has always come from his own reading, all the books that his sister brings him from the Salem Athenaeum, a private lending library, about the history of his family and city. He recalls a line from his journals: "All really educated men, whether they have studied in the halls of a university or in a cottage or a workshop, are essentially self-educated." He does not say it in this company, but will share it with Sophia on one of their walks.

It is time for Mann's lecture. All rise to get their coats. Unbeknownst to me, Sophia had been sketching me. Now she shows me what she's done, then folds her sketchbook and whisks it upstairs. I'm so startled by how far my hairline has receded that I don't look carefully at my own face.

Horace Mann became the father of public education in the United States by visiting thousands of schools and writing reports that Mary, not yet his wife, generously volunteered to recopy and edit. Report after report after report. When Mary and Mann had their first child, Sophia said of her nephew, "I suppose his first words will be a school report." Having endured several meaningless "assessments" of Salem State, I find it hard to imagine more drab work.

But his work had meaning. It was worth it. By the time he left his position, in 1848, to fill the congressional seat left vacant by the death of John Quincy Adams, Mann had established the public education system in Massachusetts, and several other states were busy building a public school system modeled on his example. There would be no going back.

I read Hawthorne and feel the heaviness of the city's bricks, coated with history and ambiguity and soot. I read about Mann's work, and breathe the possibilities of Emerson, ache with the birthing of new generations. The writer and the reformer, wrestling the past, sculpting the future. Both wise, both obsessed in their ways, both married into perhaps the most impressive Salem family ever, a family of modest means, but remarkably talented women.

Just down the block from the Peabody House, Hawthorne's statue stands on a grassy island between streets, absorbing the weather. He, like Mann, looks confident, sure of himself, despite the oblivious traffic angling past him.

Mann sits in a brightly lit room, his name attached to schools throughout the country, though, like the street names in Salem that mark the city's ancestors, few know who he was, or what he did. Handsome, but yellowing, he staunchly surveys what he has wrought.

School Reports

All great acquisition comes from voluntary thought.
—Elizabeth Peabody

When I visit a ninth-grade class at Lynn Technical High School, we need to meet in the school library, since a student just vomited in the classroom. I have them sit in a circle and I read some poems. They don't seem especially interested, though the librarian behind her counter seems appreciative. It doesn't feel like it's going well, so I reach into my bag of tricks and prepare to recite a slangy poem about basketball, one I know from memory. "This is the poem of mine that's probably closest to rap," I say, desperate.

"Rap? What's that?" a Latino ninth grader says to me, straight-faced. He's been one of the interested ones, a talker.

I pull up for a second. Did I see him smile? I smile. I catch my breath. What do I know of today's music? Does rap still exist?

"You know," I say—his words are an education—"I'm not really sure what rap is anymore. You probably know more than me. You could tell me."

He's silent, but not defiantly so. I go on.

Later, I attempt a writing exercise with them. I talk about the distinction between concrete and abstract language, and how lots of poets try, in Emily Dickinson's words, "to give abstractions shape" by imagining an abstraction as something tangible—Hope is a bird, for instance. I read them my poem about Sorrow playing right field for the Red Sox, we make a list of abstractions on the untrustworthy chalkboard that's been wheeled in for me, and then I ask them to try a poem of their own, working with one of the abstractions that we named.

The exercise was a bit rushed, but I was still disappointed in the students' inability to understand it. Only two or three of the class of twenty got the concept. Many of them came up to me and asked me to read their poems with the question, "Is this right?" I'd read a poem heavy with abstractions and oozing sentiment.

"Well, it's not really what I asked you to do, but it's fine," I'd say. "I'm glad you're writing."

They would look at me, completely confused. Was it right? Did they do it correctly? And if not, their faces seemed to ask, how could I say it was "fine"? I'm not sure what was more troubling, their inability to understand the assignment, or their concern with doing a poem "right."

"All ideas outside the book were contraband articles," wrote Horace Mann on his own education. It was something he hoped to change.

"Buckle Down" reads the cover of the MCAS workbook on the desk of the tenth-grade teacher at Lynn English High School. The MCAS (Massachusetts Comprehensive Assessment System) tests are the controversial high stakes standardized tests that have become the measuring stick for public schools and the gatekeeper for high school graduation in Massachusetts. Students take the major versions of the test in fourth, eighth, and tenth grades. They must pass the tenth-grade test to receive a high school diploma.

Around me dark-skinned kids and a few light-skinned European immigrants wait, a bit nervously, for the class to begin. I am a guest lecturer, there to read some poems and talk about poetry.

Like death, poetry is a great equalizer. I meet with what has been designated a low-level class—these kids weren't going to college— and with a few honors classes. In general, the "average" kids pick up more. When I read Yusef Komunyakaa's poem, "Venus's Flytraps," they understand the lines, "One afternoon I saw what a train did to a cow" and "My momma says I'm a mistake." They note the surprise of "I wonder what death tastes like."

I have a photo from that class that the teacher took with a digital camera and printed in black and white. I'm in the center of a group of tenth graders, standing behind a table, grinning a bit stupidly, perhaps a little too openly happy. I don't have my usual bad posture, my shoulders hunching toward my chest. Instead, I seem propped up by the students around me. The fingers of my right hand appear on the shoulder of a smiling, heavy-set white kid in a denim jacket. My left elbow hangs on the shoulder of a Latino with a baseball cap on backward and crossed arms. He's smiling, too. The kids are mostly my size, though some are already taller. There are far more boys than girls, almost all black or Latino. Probability tells me that one or two might make it to college, if that. Who?

Let my children go. As soon as my elder son entered kindergarten, I heard the drumbeat of standardized testing, distant but audible. At the school's first parent-teacher organization meeting I attended, they discussed fund-raising and how to improve MCAS scores.

When I look at the MCAS tests, I'm heartbroken. Here's the prompt for an essay question on a recent fourth-grade language arts exam:

> You woke up one morning and learned that it was snowing. School was closed for the day! It was a dream come true. Suddenly you had time to take a break from the usual routine and do what you wanted to do.
>
> Write a story about a snow day off from school that you remember. Give enough details in your story to show what you did and how wonderful the day was.

Where to begin? First, let's wince at the vague "learned that it was snowing." Isn't "saw" more accurate, cleaner? Then, let's groan at the weight of the clichés in the rest of the paragraph: "dream come true," "time to take a break," "usual routine." And isn't "usual routine" redundant?

The second paragraph: "Write a story about a snow day off from school that you remember." Will fourth graders (or even adults), seeing the word "story," assume they are supposed to write fiction or nonfiction? I suspect more will lean toward fiction—they may have heard that an essay is nonfiction, a story is fiction—and the first paragraph implies that the experience is to be imagined. So, they prepare to write fiction, but now it must be about what they "remember," to tell about what they "did." Hmm. Are they supposed to tell the truth or not? It sounds like they should write about what really happened, but isn't that an essay? A fourth grader could be stymied by such poor wording. And, as critics of this question have pointed out, what if students have never experienced a snow day? Who writes this stuff?

Apart from the writing, there's another problem, the problem of assumptions. Who says a snow day is a "dream come true" for kids? For kids whose parent or parents work, the day could well be difficult and tedious. The secretary in my department used to bring her kids in to the office, where they would read or play video games for eight hours. Yippee!

Even more troubling than the question's assumptions about

stay-at-home mothers with hot chocolate and SUVs are its assumptions about school itself. Implicit in the question is that school is not a fun place to be, so missing it is "a dream come true." Yes, with or without tests, a school day can be drab, but why enforce that idea on an exam every public-school child in the state must take? Both my sons like Horace Mann Elementary. Of course, they haven't taken the MCAS tests yet.

I wish that essay question was an aberration, but on that same exam is the poem "Homework," by the fine children's writer, Jane Yolen. "Homework" has a child speaker who intends to do various disagreeable things—cleaning the litter box, taking out the garbage—to avoid her homework. Each stanza in the poem suggests that school, and the homework it requires, is unpleasant, something that we do out of obligation, out of compliance. It is followed by a series of enervating questions that seem designed to prove this point:

> You can tell that this selection is a poem because it is
> A. short and funny.
> B. written about children.
> C. written in verse and contains rhyme.
> D. written in simple language.

To the final question, "*What is the theme of 'Homework'?*," a kid might reasonably answer: Learning sucks.

The MCAS tests—indeed, most tests—do more harm than good. They make troubling presumptions about human nature, and their high profile tends to force these presumptions on people to make them believable. Standardized tests, at least in their current incarnation, in which they are used to reward and punish schools, teachers, and students, imply that humans respond to the most basic and dull Skinnerian prompts: see candy, push lever; push lever, avoid electric shock. Am I doing this right? Have I made it to New Orleans? Push lever, push lever.

When did I realize this? It was not from my own testing experience. I never would have gotten into an Ivy League college without my SATs. And, surprisingly, it wasn't from having children and envisioning their educations—school can be deadening with or without tests if one worksheet follows the next. No, it has been from teaching at Salem State, teaching working-class students who—in class—are clearly bright, and who—out of class—are clearly wiser than students I taught at supposedly "elite" private universities.

My students' work at Salem State is often sloppy; sometimes it doesn't get turned in. Several students each semester, including some of the best, don't make it through to the end. But these problems, I have come to realize, are because the students are constantly forced to make choices, to weigh each part of their lives and decide which to put down and which to shoulder.

I was speaking recently to an adjunct faculty member at the college who would be teaching for the first time. She ran by me her idea for her opening composition assignment: she was going to give her class a few articles about George W. Bush's proposed exploration of Mars and ask them to write a paper about whether it was a good idea or not. I thought about it. It wasn't a topic I would have chosen, but why? I imagined student responses. At an "elite" school," most of the students would have launched right into the assignment. *Here's what the country should do! I have the answer.*

At Salem State, the student response would be much different. Most would feel awkward about writing such a paper, partly because they have not always been encouraged to believe that their opinion counts, and partly because they would humbly realize—in a way that more privileged students wouldn't—that they don't know nearly enough to be able to say anything intelligent about the question. This recognition lies in a wisdom that students at more prestigious colleges lack. What the hell do any of us know about the exploration of Mars? Although they might not be able to articulate it, my students would comprehend the artificiality of the assignment, and, implicitly, they would question its significance. Should they ask for time off work and lose out on some seemingly necessary cash to do a good job on the paper, a paper about outer space? What to shoulder?

The classroom in Horace Mann Elementary School in Salem is dark when I step into it. A flash—a mouse (Horace Mann's mouse?)—scurries across the floor and disappears. I'm here to talk to my son's third-grade class about poetry. Soon, the light flicks on, and the children march in, bands of paper around their heads. They are magnets, with an N and an S on either side of the bands. They are, at their teacher's command, repelling or attracting each other. When they repel, they stand with arms folded, staring sternly at another student a few feet away, or they have their back turned to another. When they attract, they put hands on each other's shoulders.

I'm introduced, and, after I ask their names, I begin talking to them about imagination. What do they think of when I say that word? Purple dogs. A rubber chicken dancing on a plate. I talk about Wallace Stevens, how he felt the imagination works with reality, how the ordinary, the everyday, like a snowman or a blackbird, can be amazing and surprising. "There are many truths," I say, quoting Stevens. The students list some ordinary things—an eraser, a chalkboard, the ceiling—and I read them a poem about muffins that my college students composed: "Ten Ways of Looking at a Muffin." Then I take some scissors and hold them up—"How about these? What do these make you think of?"

And they're off: it's a person who is always talking. It's tired of eating paper all day. It's an alligator. I can hardly rein them in.

A few minutes later, we break them into small groups, and they're off again. In the group I work with, Aaron asks if he can do a poem of his own about an eraser. He already has "got some" for it. I want to say yes, but we're on task. "Later. Let's do a clock now. Everyone try and come up with some things." Aaron walks across the room and curls up behind an easel, composing his own ways to look at a clock. His writing, it turns out, is so rudimentary that he can't read what he wrote. The words are far from how they are spelled: K-l-o-k. But he lists ten ways, numbered and all. ("Amazing," his teacher tells me later.) The clock looks like a marble, he says, the clock is like a head, a balloon floating in the sky, the clock is the world.

When we gather together, we listen to the poems each group has composed. Here's one by Aidan, Daniel, Shanteliz, and Yanisha:

A Spoon

A spoon could be a metal teardrop for the Tin Man.

A spoon is like an asteroid on a stick.

A spoon is a weird mirror that makes you look upside down.

It can be a teeter-totter for food.

Or a catapult for banana wars.

A metal diving board.

A tool to eat poisonous food that may not touch your hands.

A drill to make a hole in a wall of mashed potatoes.

A shovel to dig up a dog's bone.

A gavel in a courtroom.

A reflex hammer to break a tiny house in fruitland.

A sled for George.

A balance beam for a baby chick.

It could be an upside-down snake.

Something to grow flowers on.

A mirror to check your teeth.

An umbrella at the beach for an ant.

A periscope to spy on people.

A spoon is the pencil with which I wrote this poem.

We all applaud after each poem, and the groups take questions and comments. Then, I answer some questions about poetry, about being a writer and a teacher. We have to stop before I can answer them all. It's time for lunch.

I am failing these children. I'm encouraging them to think that there are not right answers, only interesting ones—a clock isn't one thing; it can be many. Although I dropped the word *metaphor* into the discussion a few times, I'm not teaching them the word *verse* or *stanza*, or that poetry rhymes, all of which are expectations for the MCAS. In fact, they're discovering that poems don't necessarily rhyme, that poems can be lies, that poems can be fun, that school and learning can be joyful. Or, to put it another way, using something ordinary from their lives: school is like a magnet; it can repel, or it can attract.

The Shore

I love the notion of living near the dead.
—Sophia Peabody

I have lived in Salem for almost eight years, longer than I have in any other place. My sons have ground the city's dirt into their knees and elbows diving for baseballs. They have swallowed some of its dust. My wife can find most yard sales without a map. The absence of street signs amuses rather than annoys. The city has become home.

The college, too, has become home. When I hear that in a recent study Massachusetts ranks forty-ninth in the nation in spending for public higher education, I grimace, but I don't send out my résumé. My students are trapped in a state that, ironically—given Horace Mann's legacy—scorns public education on every level. The children of Chestnut Street are whisked off to private schools before kindergarten. When they are teens, they meet with tutors, angling for higher SAT scores. The kids at my son's school ride a bus to an old, poorly lit Salem State gym because their school doesn't have its own gymnasium. Their aged building is, according to the superintendent, barely adequate. And by the time some of these public-school students enroll at Salem State College, they have endured years of the world telling them—based on standardized test scores and empty pockets—that they are barely adequate. The students from private schools fear and pity them. It amounts to a psychological war.

How the past echoes! In her loving biography of her husband, *Life of Horace Mann*, Mary writes about an early convention on education that Mann held in Salem, one that did not go well: "One gentleman, who made one of the first speeches, questioned the expediency of endeavoring to get the educated classes to patronize public schools. He spoke, he said, in the interests of mothers who preferred private schools for their children; and he believed the reasons that they had would always prevail: they would have their children grow up in intimacies with those of their own class. No one spoke on the American side of this question."

It is February 2004. I am walking the icy streets of Salem. I want to feel the spirit of Horace Mann, the one I sensed in the school that bears his name, the one where third graders wrote me a class thank-you poem about a heart: "A heart," my son contributed, "is a bouncy ball. I played with it yesterday." But whether it is the chill of the winter, or the ghost of the MCAS tests, or the fact that Mann, despite his bust, was just a visitor here, it is Hawthorne's spirit that haunts, with his doubts about improving human nature, his sense that this city, old even in Hawthorne's day, drains creativity. It is Hawthorne, not Mann, who is Salem's ghost, he who wrote about it. Though he finally fled the city, his is the name of the city's main hotel. There are Hawthorne Animal Hospital; Hawthorne Cove Marina; Hawthorne Tours; Hawthorne Ear, Nose & Throat Specialists; and Hawthorne Oil.

I'm coming from the college, heading downtown to lunch with a colleague, our new Hawthorne scholar. I walk along the shoreline, trying not to look at the power plant chuffing its soot across the harbor, until I come to a secluded cove. There, just over a stone wall, I see them: five—no six—swans resting on the gravelly sand. Two are yearlings, brown feathers mixing with white. They all startle, and I stop walking. There are no boats out on the rough, cold waves, but mallards are everywhere in the surf before me. They gambol like children in the polluted water. The swans flutter back to a rest, orange beaks bright against their papery necks. Their webbed feet are half-buried in the sand and broken glass and damp paper scraps; their bodies hover above it all, like glorious ideas.

If there are such things as ghosts, let these be them, spirits of the company I kept in the Peabodys' parlor back in 1838. The tourists will never see their grace, the political hacks on the Board of Education will never know how rich they make this gritty world.

But let these be simply swans, too, soon to fly north to a secluded lake somewhere far from here. Let their children be born elsewhere. *There are many truths.*

I keep walking, and the swans let me pass. Eventually, I veer away from the harbor, end up in front of 53 Charter Street, the Peabody House. Although it qualifies for one, it has no commemorative plaque. The owner, a descendant of the Peabodys, has allowed the outside to deteriorate, apparently to spite the city. Rumor says it is beautiful inside. The day has wavered between clouds and sun, but now it has gone as gray as the house. A few raindrops. Those nights when he first felt the stirrings of love, Hawthorne might have stood where I stand, having taken leave of Sophia and her sisters, perhaps after walking them home from Mann's lecture. In the darkness he senses but cannot see the grave of his great-great-grandfather, the name carved firmly and exactly, as befitting such a prestigious man.

He sighs, and his mind turns to the evening he has just spent—all this talk of education, Sophia's friendly eye. The lights are on in the Peabody House. Shadows cross the curtains. For a moment, he could be any man in love, hopeful for his future, however vague its outlines.

Horace Mann did not drink, smoke, or use foul language, yet he was on to something. Friends thought him foolish for forsaking money. At the age of fifty-three, when he was a U.S. congressman, he had the opportunity to become governor and perhaps president. Instead, he passed on these conventional ambitions and took the position of college president out in the boonies of Ohio at a school that was just opening, a school that in 1853 was one of the first coed schools in the country, Antioch College. Yes, like Hawthorne, he left Massachusetts, but he also stayed put—committing himself to learning and teaching, often against long odds. He and Mary Mann wrote the wisest words I have ever read about education: "In a republic like ours, children must be educated . . . so as to be above pride as well as above abasement."

Neither man is wrong. Hawthorne said goodbye to the city and spent much of the rest of his life in Europe. He concludes "The Custom House" by writing of his "decapitation" as a Customs House officer, his removal from office when a new administration was voted into Washington. "The moment when a man's head drops off is seldom or never, I am inclined to think, precisely the most agreeable of his life," he writes, but for him, it was a blessing. It freed him from Salem, and it freed him to write again. He had to leave his civil life to renew his writing life.

What to shoulder? Am I losing myself in the whirlpool of the classroom? In the heaviness of Salem, its thick past and ignorant present? Didn't I, like the young Hawthorne, dream of being a poet? Across the street, the wall of Yin Yu Tang is as white as an absolute answer. I pull my gloveless hands from my pockets and grasp the black iron fence surrounding the Charter Street Cemetery. Depending on the angle from which you view me, I look like either a prisoner dreaming escape or an outsider hoping for entry. What I see, though, are only my own hands, curled and cold, scarred from basketball at the Salem Y—all those hands groping for a ball for . . . for what? These hands that hold chalk, that mark student papers and poems, chapped and wrinkled at the knuckles. I hardly recognize them.

At my feet, the red line needs repainting. Perhaps, though, it would be better if it just disappeared, gradually flaking off onto our soles, then falling off them, too, somewhere. The specks would land where they land, traveling with each new step, each rain, mapping a new path impossible to see or follow. It is an imaginary path of course, but it spans the distance from the brick sidewalks of Chestnut Street to the marijuana butts in High Street Park, from China to Charter Street to Salem State. The path even stretches through the doors of my son's elementary school, past the kindergarteners' self-portraits, to the bust of Mann, that old gift sitting among books and children and mice, eyes perpetually open.

What Is

To Nancy D. Harrington, 12th President of Salem State College

So many fabricated ghosts
in this old city
of imaginary hauntings.
What of what is? What of

the boy from the preschool
smearing his chocolaty hands
on your sky-blue dress
at the Earth Day celebration?

That was our son. Those children
surrounding you, cake-smeared faces
and hands, those were our sons
and daughters, and you stood

among them. That day,
and these years, you have moved
out from behind the podium
to stand among them, among us,

out from behind the presidential seal.
No microphone, words unamplified,
no script—this is improvised,
shaped by fifty years: reading

to fifth graders, speaking
to neighbors about dorms
and traffic, telling legislators
not to cut our budget

again. No script,
no cell phone, no email,
no podium, standing straight,
legs planted, looking

at us, at Salem State.
You've been looking out for us.
So that, as you stand there,
one person speaking to others,

professing faith in our minds,
our words, our deeds, we know
you speak the truth because you know us.
You have been us. You are us.

You are what is. A sixteen-year-old
student in 1956, here because
your father died and the family
couldn't afford the school

your sister attended.
So you came to this place
that has been here since 1854,
that has anchored the city in the years

when wars reared, when leather
disappeared . . . Beyond the myths
and the murders, beyond Hawthorne
and 1692, what of what is?

What of the Sylvania Plant
where the community
came to work, to make light bulbs,
and what of when the work left,

and the buildings sat like
empty, cracked shells,
on the city's shore?
Those families have returned

to those same buildings
as students. You filled
that shell of a place
with books, and music, and food,

and smart classrooms and, yes,
parking spaces and grass
and air-conditioned dorms.
President for seventeen years—

the span from infancy to college.
What a wondrous child you've raised!
And now you send her off on her own,
still growing, still learning,

but firm on her feet.
You stepped out from behind
the podium and into Salem,
from the preschool on the ridge

above Forest River,
to the muck at Cat Cove.
No microphone, Salem State blue
dress, at a community event

to save the planet.
Think of that chocolate
as a sweet kiss of thanks.
It can't be washed away.

THE DIAMOND

"In short, human weakness and strength, passion and policy, Man's tendencies, his aims and modes of pursuing them, his individual character, and his character in the mass, may be studied almost as well here as on the theatre of nations; and with this great advantage, that, be the lesson ever so disastrous, its Lilliputian scope still makes the beholder smile."

—Nathaniel Hawthorne, from "The Sister Years," first published in *The Salem Gazette*, 1839.

Racist

"That team's racist," said KJ, staring hard into the Topsfield dugout. The teams had finished their warmups and crowded into their respective dugouts, while the two head coaches stood with the umpire at home plate, reviewing the ground rules. Kenny looked through the chain-link at the Topsfield players in their royal blue uniforms, standing in clumps talking to each other. One kid snuck up behind another and squirted water on his neck.

"What did they say?" Kenny asked.

"Just look at them," said Julian, the only eleven-year-old on Salem's tournament team.

Kenny looked again. The Topsfield team was all white. Then again, Julian was white. Kenny was white. Half of Salem's team was white. KJ, Giancarlo, and the rest, except for Jesse Lopes, who said he was black though his mom was white, were Spanish from the Dominican Republic.

Topsfield's white kids, though, weren't like Salem's white kids. They were the tall kids that Kenny played against in AAU, kids who had floppy blond hair and talked about "the ghetto," who mocked other teams for wearing their shirts tucked in, who mocked each other when one of them screwed up.

"Hey, Kenny. Good luck today." Coach Viera, the Peabody coach, was standing behind the caged dugout, his hands in the pockets of his crisp white shorts. He wore a navy-blue collared shirt with "Peabody LL" stenciled over the heart and a navy Peabody cap.

"Thanks, Coach," Kenny said.

Everyone knew Coach Viera, or "Coach V," and Kenny felt a twinge of pride that Coach V had said "hi" to him. In addition to playing for Salem's tournament team, Kenny played on the elite AAU team run by Coach V, the Angels.

Kenny was the only Salem kid who had played AAU, a competitive travel league separate from Little League. It cost almost 2000 dollars, but Kenny's dad had said it was worth it. "Guys who play AAU get college scholarships." Kenny's dad had played in high school with Coach Viera, and last fall he had talked to Coach V about Kenny joining the Angels, the AAU team based in Peabody. Kenny had been excited when Coach

V said yes. He loved the idea of playing in college. Maybe he could even get drafted. Peabody baseball was legendary. Their Little League all-stars had won the district the last four years. In 2014 they won the state and nearly got to the Little League World Series. When Kenny was younger and played in all-star tournaments, Peabody would crush Salem; they would crush everyone.

AAU didn't have the drama of the Little League tournament, though. The tournament was about city pride, the all-stars from every city competing against each other for a chance to go to Williamsport, Pennsylvania, and be on national TV; AAU was about personal ambition. Even though the competition was great, the AAU doubleheaders on Saturday and Sunday were exhausting, and it didn't really matter whether you won or lost. Still, Kenny liked learning the game. Coach V knew baseball. He had shown Kenny how to hide his curve ball and how to throw a slider that actually slid. And it was cool to play with Peabody players. They didn't screw around. When Kenny threw a ball hard, he knew they'd catch it. Kenny thought Coach V should have batted him fourth or fifth, rather than seventh, but, Kenny's dad said, "You're playing. You're pitching. You're learning how baseball should be played. Stay with these guys and you'll be playing in college. I don't think Coach V has ever taken a Salem kid on the Angels."

Coach V lifted his cap off his head and wiped his forehead with his sleeve, then ran his hand through his short dark hair. He was deeply tanned from being on the field all summer, probably darker than anyone on Salem's team. What did it mean to be white, Kenny thought. Coach V was nothing like the Topsfield players.

"Gonna be a hot one," Coach V said, "keep drinking water."

"Gotcha, Coach." He turned back to the field. It figured that Coach V would be at this game, scouting his future opposition. Peabody was always a step or two ahead of the rest of the teams. Kenny wondered what it would be like to play against Coach V. Maybe, if Salem actually did well, he'd get a chance. First, Topsfield.

KJ came up to Kenny, flung one arm over his shoulder and pointed at the Topsfield players with the other one, "Yo, homeboy," he said, "We kick their ass. They can't touch you." Kenny nodded. The district tournament was about to begin.

This was the year, finally, when Salem was supposed to make noise in the tournament. If they could get past Peabody, they would even have a shot at winning the state title. "Two and screw," was how things usually went for Salem. They'd play two games, lose two games, and it would be over. But this year the stars had aligned. Giancarlo, a stocky Spanish kid, had moved to Salem from the Bronx at the beginning of the season, and he was the best pitcher in the area. Kenny had only gotten one hit off him in the regular season, and Kenny could hit. Kenny was a strong number two pitcher, and together they could carry the team a long way. And then there was KJ, their second baseman.

KJ didn't look like much. Skinny, with black curly hair that flattened out on sweaty days, he wasn't one of those twelve-year-olds, like Kenny, who were a head taller than everyone else, but he was impossible to get out. He was so quick out of the box that he simply had to hit the ball on the ground to get on. And once he reached base, look out. Kenny had watched ESPN shows about Jackie Robinson, how he would rattle pitchers and steal home. KJ was like that, dancing far off the base, always daring the catcher to pick him off. If the catcher threw behind him, he'd just zip to the next base. If the catcher tried to ignore him and flipped the ball back to the pitcher softly, KJ would still take off. Catcher and pitcher—every player in the field—had to be on high alert whenever KJ got on the base path.

Your only hope to get KJ out was to strike him out, but that never happened. Even Giancarlo couldn't get his fastball past him. KJ would rev up for a fastball on every pitch, and so he would get around on anything—you couldn't jam him. But throw him a curve and, even if you fooled him completely and got him way out in front, he'd still make contact, chop the ball to third or short, and beat it out by five steps. Usually, the fielder wouldn't even bother throwing.

And you couldn't pitch him away either. Because he'd be so jacked up to swing, he'd crowd the plate so he could smack anything on the outside corner. It was a puzzle Kenny couldn't solve. No one could. KJ would score nearly every time he came to the plate.

Kenny had asked about getting KJ to play on his AAU team, but Kenny's dad said that KJ wouldn't be as good once he got older and played on the big diamond. He was too scrawny.

"Why not let him try?" Kenny asked, "Could you talk to Coach V?" But Kenny's dad just shook his head.

Kenny was excited to be playing with KJ, instead of against him. In Salem's city league, Kenny had played on the Cubs, and KJ and Giancarlo had played on the rival Cardinals. Now, they got to play together to represent Salem. KJ's mom, who spoke more Spanish than English, had become one of Kenny's biggest fans. She called him "gran hombre" and KJ "hombrecito."

This year, thanks to KJ and Giancarlo, the Cardinals had won the Salem city league, which meant that the Salem tournament team's coach would be the Cardinals' coach, Coach Frank. Coach Frank was another reason that it seemed Salem's chances were good. Coach Frank was not a legend like Coach V, but at least he wasn't a typical clueless Salem coach. Kenny didn't really like Coach Frank because he lorded over the rest of the Salem league, and because he always managed to beat Kenny's team, but everyone, including Kenny, believed he was the best coach in the city, the only one who really knew baseball. Before the morning bell at the middle school, players on Frank's team would complain about his extra sliding practices at the beach or the way he yelled at a kid, and Kenny would feel envious. Sure, Coach Frank was a screamer—Kenny liked how Coach V never yelled in AAU—but Frank's teams were always good.

It turned out to be true. Salem had a good team, a damn good team. Topsfield couldn't touch Kenny or Giancarlo, and KJ ran around the bases like no one was in the field. They won two more before they lost a tight one to Danvers, but the loss just seemed to make them more focused. Even though Giancarlo blew out his arm (Kenny's dad said that Coach Frank made him throw too many curves) and would have to watch from the bench, they won two more easily and suddenly they were facing Peabody in the championship.

As they had rolled along, racking up the wins, Kenny took extra pleasure in defeating the all-white teams. He recognized some of their best players from AAU, and he knew that now they would remember him, and remember KJ and Giancarlo, and remember Salem.

As the players and coaches stood along the baselines and held their caps over their hearts for the national anthem, Kenny looked over at the

Peabody team. They were all white, but they didn't feel white like the other teams. For one thing, Coach V and his assistant coaches looked like they lived in a tanning salon. And Peabody's team was mostly Italian, all their names ending in vowels. They weren't like the other white teams on the North Shore, full of kids who skied and used their phones in the dugout. Those white kids lived in huge houses with long driveways, the ones that Kenny would see on woodsy back roads going to AAU games, houses that were barely visible, set behind stone walls and trees.

Peabody players grew up in ordinary houses like Kenny's. They were sons of cops and firefighters. Their fathers bought them the most juiced bats the league allowed, and they had the gear and style of the pros. They gripped their batting gloves in their fists when they were on the base paths; they wore eye black and covered their mouths with their gloves when they had conferences on the mound. They took the game seriously.

And they were impressively, even irritatingly, professional and respectful. When Kenny had ripped a double against them in the tourney game last year, the shortstop had said, "Nice hit." When a Salem player got frustrated and flung a bat or helmet, they didn't smirk, even though they would be winning by ten runs.

The anthem ended, and Salem shuffled into their dugout. They seemed timid. Were they thinking of all the times Peabody had destroyed them when they were younger? A few of them were pointing out Gino, the Peabody pitcher, who Kenny played with on the Angels. "He's a monster," one said. Kenny wanted to say something, but this wasn't about words. They needed to prove they could compete. He stepped out of the dugout to where KJ was taking his practice swings.

"You get us started, right?"

"No doubt," KJ said, popping his bubble gum, "and you finish it."

KJ strutted to the plate. He held up one hand to the ump as he dug a small gully in the batter's box, the way he always did to brace his back foot. Then he stepped all the way in, windmilled his bat twice, pointed it at the pitcher, and got into his stance.

"Play ball," the umpire hollered, bringing his mask down.

Kenny looked across at Coach V, squatting next to the entrance of his dugout. How would he try to pitch to KJ? Coach V made a fist, then touched three fingers to his cap. Same signals that the Angels used. Fastball high and inside. They wanted to brush KJ back early. Get him off the plate; make him worry about getting hit. The pitch came in, and KJ pulled his chest back just a few inches and lifted his chin. Kenny smiled. KJ's feet hadn't moved. He wasn't going anywhere.

"Ball one."

"You got this," Kenny said.

Coach V called for a curve ball, outside corner. The pitcher threw, and KJ leaned across the plate and ripped a shot down the third base line, half a foot foul.

Coach V had done what he wanted, Kenny knew. He was going to come high and tight again, tie KJ up, make him swing late, only KJ never swung late.

Sure enough—fastball inside corner, Coach V signaled. The pitch came in, and KJ scorched it, a line drive that shot so hard at the left fielder that he had trouble fielding it on the short hop and it ricocheted off his glove a few feet to his side. KJ didn't blink, shooting for second when he saw the bobble, and the left fielder hurried the throw—offline. Safe by a mile.

Salem's bench went wild, rattling the chain link in front of the dugout. They could hit these guys. They could play with Peabody.

KJ wasn't through. When the pitcher bounced the ball in the dirt, he took third easily. The catcher didn't even try a throw. Kenny moved to the edge of the dugout. As usual, he was batting third, after Julian. Julian popped the next pitch to the first baseman. One out. In the third base coach's box, Coach Frank leaned forward and said a few words to KJ. Kenny looked down at Coach Frank for a signal, though he knew there would be no signal. He just needed to rip the ball.

And he did. A rocket—but right at the second baseman. The crowd oohed, but it hadn't accomplished anything. Two out, and KJ still on third. Was this going to be the same old story—they couldn't catch a break against Peabody? You make your own breaks, Kenny's dad always said, but damn.

Kenny picked up his glove, waiting for the third out, starting to feel a little queasy about facing the Peabody lineup. He knew the first five batters. He'd played with all of them on the Angels. They would be an ordeal.

The first pitch to Jesse Lopes, Salem's fourth batter, was high, but he swung anyway. And missed by a mile. "Make him pitch to you!" Kenny yelled.

Before throwing the ball back to the pitcher, the catcher stared at KJ, who was dancing far off the bag. Kenny wanted to warn KJ. Peabody's pitcher, Gino, liked to grab the toss from his catcher barehanded and whip it to third to pick off runners. KJ could get nailed if he wasn't careful. Kenny started to yell, but it was too late. The catcher flipped the ball and there was Gino, barehanding it and gunning it to third.

Only KJ hadn't gone back. He'd dashed home as soon as he saw Gino shift his feet. He slid in with a grand explosion of dirt, which seemed as though it had been set off by the screams of the Salem players. 1-0!

KJ jumped up, pulled off his helmet, and jogged to the dugout. His face was stony, but his tongue flicked from one side of his mouth to the other. The players pounded him on the back and slapped his hand.

When Jesse struck out, it hardly mattered. Kenny was so pumped he had to stop himself from running out to the mound. He walked, like the pros did. This was going to be a fucking game.

Kenny wasn't sure how he did it, but he struck out the first two batters. Gino smashed an opposite field double against him, but he jammed their number four hitter just enough so that he flied out to right. Salem went 1-2-3 the next inning, but Kenny gave up a walk, a passed ball, and a two-out bloop single and the game was tied. That walk!

In the third, Salem's 8th and 9th batters both looked bad striking out. They couldn't hit the curve, and they couldn't catch up with the fastball. Then, KJ came up. Coach V kept signaling curveballs at the knees. Kenny knew where this was going. Even if these pitches worked, and KJ didn't hit the ball hard, he'd ground it to third or short and beat the throw.

And that's what he did—a chopper to the third baseman, who rushed in, then rushed the throw, sailing it over first base. KJ was on second, and Salem's dugout was howling. Standing on second with his hands on his hips, KJ blew a huge bubble, like he couldn't be more relaxed. Gino's first pitch to Julian was high, and KJ rushed off the base. The catcher took a few steps toward him until KJ hopped back—just one step—toward second. He was like a bird.

"Give me the ball!" Gino said, his eyes darting back and forth between KJ and the catcher.

"Don't watch the runner," Coach V yelled. "Catch the ball first!" Was there a little nervousness in Coach V's voice? He sounded different somehow—a little angry, like Coach Frank.

Gino took the throw from the catcher and quickly grabbed the ball with his throwing hand, threatening to throw to second. KJ just stared at him, mouth open, ready to bolt back.

"Just get on the rubber," Coach V growled. He *was* angry.

Gino kept glancing at KJ, and his next three pitches to Julian were all off target. A walk. He was rattled, and the Salem bench banged on the dugout fence, screaming their heads off. Kenny took a deep breath and walked to the plate. One of Peabody's coaches had gone out to talk with Gino. Then he jogged back and said something to Coach V. Kenny put one foot in the batter's box and looked toward Coach Frank in the coach's box at third. Really, though, he was sneaking a glance at Coach V. Kenny's dad hated it when other teams tried to steal signs when Kenny pitched. "Not at this level," he'd say, "'cause it's not like you can retaliate. No one's going to throw at a kid to send a message. That's what they do in high school or college. Throw one right in the batter's ear. You'll see when you get there."

Coach V made a fist and touched his chest. Kenny bit his lip so he wouldn't grin. Fastball down the middle! Coach V must think Kenny would be taking the first pitch, and he wanted to get Gino back on track. Or maybe he thought that Kenny wasn't really that good. Fastball down the middle.

Kenny didn't quite get all of it, but he got more than enough. The ball soared over the right center fence, plunking down on the back row of the bleachers and arcing into the air like a fountain.

Kenny had hit home runs before. He had two in AAU this year, and he led the Salem Little League with nine, but this one felt different. Maybe it was the big crowd, maybe it was hearing his father whoop, or KJ's mother cry out "gran hombre" over and over, maybe it was how his teammates raised their voices and rushed out to meet him at home plate. Maybe it was the way Coach Frank slapped his ass hard as he rounded third, or the stricken look on Coach V's face. This homer mattered, just like KJ's steal of home had mattered. It mattered to Salem, old "two-and-screw" Salem. Kenny jumped on the plate with both feet and was engulfed by his teammates. KJ had his hand on Kenny's helmet as they moved in a mob toward the dugout and kept yelling in his ear, "We got this, bro! We got this!"

"Second time through. Now you've seen him, you'll hit him," Coach V hollered from the 3rd base box as Kenny stepped on the rubber to start the third. Kenny glanced over at his AAU coach. Was Coach V trying to rattle him? But Coach V kept his face on his batter.

"Second time through. Just like the first time!" KJ shouted from behind him. Kenny stepped off the rubber and looked out at KJ. KJ pointed at him and pounded his chest twice. Kenny smiled. He wanted to look over at Coach V, but he didn't dare.

The second batter pulled a fastball over the left field fence, but Kenny got through the inning with just that one run, though he walked two guys after the homer. 4-2. It was going to be tight. He couldn't give up any more runs. And maybe he and KJ could sneak another run or two across the next time they came up.

Salem didn't score in the fourth, and, thanks to a nice backhand scoop by Carlos at third and a sweet running catch by Julian in center, neither did Peabody. Kenny thought Coach Frank looked anxious. He wasn't barking at players, like he usually did, and he actually raised his fist triumphantly when Julian put the inning away with his catch. Salem had never been this close to winning the district.

The fifth. Like the third, Salem's eighth and ninth batters went down easy, and then KJ came up. KJ would get to second, no doubt, and then, if Julian could get on, Kenny could do more damage. KJ went through his usual routine, windmilling his bat and pointing it at Gino.

Kenny peeked at Coach V. He had been too wrapped up in the game to look over at the signs, and he'd felt a little guilty about stealing the sign on his home run, but now he was curious how Coach V would deal with KJ.

Coach V made a cutting motion with his hand, like a judo chop.

It was a sign that Kenny had never seen before.

The catcher set up inside, nearly directly behind KJ. The pitcher fired, and a fastball shot right into KJ's rib. The pitch landed like a punch, a hollow thud that made it sound as if the ball had somehow punctured the skin.

KJ collapsed instantly, and there were gasps from the bleachers, then an eerie silence in which Kenny could hear KJ rasp through his teeth—"Fuuuuuckkk!" His eyes were squeezed shut. Kenny felt he should do something, but the adults were already in motion, making sure things were okay. Coach Frank and his assistant, Coach Cal, had both jogged out to KJ, and the umpire had taken off his mask.

Coach Cal was talking quietly to KJ. Coach Frank looked grim. Coach V walked up to them, his navy-blue shirt separating the red of the Salem coaches. "You need an ice pack, Frank?"

"We got it," said Coach Frank. Coach Cal hopped up and jogged to get the first aid kit. Kenny and some of the other Salem players came out of the dugout and crowded around.

"Guys back up. Give him room to breathe," said the umpire.

"Get back in the dugout!" Coach Frank yelled. The Salem players turned and bumped into each other squeezing back in.

In his mind, Kenny kept seeing that chopping signal. "That's fucking bullshit," he said to Jesse.

"What?" Jesse said. Some of the other Salem kids were listening in.

"He hit him on purpose."

"Really?"

Kenny nodded. He was sure of it. Through the chain-links protecting the dugout, Kenny glared at Coach V, but he was talking to the ump about the rules on a player coming out of a game due to injury.

KJ was still on the ground. Kenny could see his body rising and falling in a slowing rhythm. Finally, with Coach Frank and Coach Cal each taking him by the arm, KJ stood. The crowd applauded, the way they always did when someone got up from an injury. KJ, bent over, winced with each step.

"Maybe a broken rib," he heard Coach Cal say as the coaches eased KJ down on the dugout bench.

"It's not that bad," said KJ. "I'll go back in next inning."

"We'll see," said Frank, "keep that ice on it, and lay down as long as you need to."

Coach Frank sent Javier in to run for KJ. Javier was as fast as KJ, but he had none of KJ's instincts. He wouldn't be able to scoot his way around the bases.

As Coach Frank headed out of the dugout, Kenny grabbed his forearm. It was so thick his hand was barely able to grip it.

"Coach," he said.

"What?" Frank looked down at him.

"That—that was intentional. Isn't that illegal?"

Coach Frank stared hard at him. Kenny stared back.

"I saw Coach V give a signal for it."

"You sure?" Frank looked over at the Peabody dugout. Kenny did, too. Coach V was looking at the two of them, impassive. Frank turned back to him slowly. "I doubt that. Shit happens. Worry about the game."

He turned away and stopped to talk with Julian before jogging back to the third base box. He shook his head and said something to Coach V as he passed him.

On the second pitch to Julian, Peabody picked Javier off first base, using the play Kenny had learned on the Angels where the catcher looks like he's just going to toss the ball back to the pitcher, and then, if the runner drops his head and steps casually back to first, as Javier did, he guns him out. It's a play that takes advantage of the runner not being alert.

The pickoff fired up Peabody, and they roared into their dugout.

Kenny hated them, the whole fucking team, the way they were better and smarter than other teams, better than Salem. The way most of them played AAU, got private lessons. Sure, they weren't rich dicks like the Topsfield boys, but they were dicks, racist dicks, Kenny thought. And now they played dirty, too. KJ was Salem's heart, Salem's motor. KJ was fucking unstoppable. Unless you threw a ball into his ribs.

Kenny threw all his warm-up pitches full speed. He tried to throw harder than he'd ever done before, as if he could throw through a brick wall, but his pitches were the same speed as always, maybe even a little slower. "It's all in the motion," Coach V had taught him. "Nice and smooth. Relaxed. Let the pitch throw itself." Kenny took a deep breath and, for his last two warmups, tried to ease up, but his body felt tight, jerky. He didn't want to pitch. He wanted to fight. He'd never gotten into a fight in his life, just a few shoving matches at the middle school, but now he wanted to take a swing at someone.

First pitch. Coach Frank called for a fastball at the knees, outside corner. Kenny wasn't going outside. He zeroed in on the batter's hip, wound up nice and easy, and fired.

The ball struck right on the hip. The sound was sharper, less hollow, than when KJ had gotten hit. The Peabody kid was knocked back a step. He looked up at the sky, grimacing. Then he put his head down and wiped his eyes with his arm.

Coach V jogged down from the third base line and put his arm on the kid's shoulder. He said a few words to him. The kid nodded and wiped his eyes again, and Coach V slapped his ass and the kid jogged down to first base as the crowd applauded.

Coach V and the ump started talking. Kenny just wanted the fucking ball. Come on, he thought, Come on! He'd pitch now! He'd strike out their whole team.

The ump waved to the other ump and Coach Frank to come discuss something. When they had all gathered at home plate, Kenny heard Coach V saying, "My players" and "rule book."

Coach Frank, Kenny could see, was getting angry. He leaned in toward the ump and raised his arms, his palms facing the sky. Then the ump was talking, and Coach V chimed in.

From the stands, a guy with a raspy voice yelled, "C'mon. Keep the game moving!" A few more words, Coach Frank shaking his head, the umps doing most of the talking, and then Coach Frank walked out to the mound.

"What is it?" Kenny said.

"You're out of the game."

"What?"

"They're saying you hit the batter intentionally. The rulebook says you get thrown out."

"It slipped."

"That's what I said, but it's not my call."

Kenny looked at the ump, who was dusting off the plate. Then he looked at Coach V, who was calmly staring at him.

"This is bullshit!" Kenny said, keeping his gaze on Coach V.

"Hey," said Coach Frank. Kenny turned back to Salem's coach. "Under control. He's not going to make a big deal out of throwing you out, but you've got to go sit. It will look like we're just replacing you."

Coach V had turned to his dugout and was talking to his assistant coaches.

"Hey," said Coach Frank, louder, "Look at me!" Kenny did. "You're going to walk off this field, and you're not even going to peek at Viera. You're going to sit on the bench and keep quiet."

"But this is bullshit!" Kenny hoped Coach V could hear him.

"Don't make this about you. We got a game to win."

Kenny glared at his coach.

Coach Frank rubbed the baseball in his hands. "You pitched a helluva game. Helluva game. We got 'em scared."

From the stands, that raspy voice again—"Keep the game moving!"

Kenny put his head down. He felt like he was going to burst out crying, and he could not—could not!—let himself do that. He strode off the mound, hurrying to the dugout. The fans applauded loudly, but Kenny just wished he could walk down the first base line, out the gate, and have his father drive him home. Instead, he walked into the dugout, past KJ, who was lying on the bench, holding the ice pack to his rib, past Giancarlo, the best pitcher he'd ever seen, sitting impassive, his arm in a sling. He sat down.

Kenny felt like they were wounded soldiers, carried off the field of battle. It didn't make him feel proud or important. It made him feel helpless. He thought about his cousin, who spent four years in Afghanistan. "One big shit show," he'd said, "Don't believe no one."

He didn't want to sit. The game was still on. He hopped up and clutched the dugout fence, wrapping his fingers through it. "Jules, you got this. Nice and easy." 4-2. They still had the lead.

Julian got a ground out to first, moving the runner down to second, then gave up a double down the line that made it 4-3. He walked the next batter. Damn it. Coach V was clapping in the third base box. Kenny knew that clap from AAU. It was crazy loud, like gunshots.

The whole Peabody team was standing in their dugout. In the field, Salem players were screaming encouragement, desperation in their voices. "C'mon, Jules!" Kenny hollered. He closed his eyes for a second, trying to send some of his energy to Julian. Two more outs.

On the third pitch, the batter lifted a short fly behind first base. It was the second baseman's ball, and KJ would have had it easily, but the guy who replaced him was tentative, and Jesse Lopes, the big first baseman, called for it, backpedaling. "Jesse, you got it!" Kenny heard Jesse's mother screaming. Still backpedaling, Jesse reached over his head and the ball landed in his glove. But then he fell backward onto the outfield grass. The ball bounced out, arcing over his head and landing on his chest. Jesse flung his hands across his shirt, pinning the ball to it. The umpire signaled out, and the Salem crowd roared.

"Jesse! You the man!" Kenny screamed. Still on the ground, Jesse clutched the ball and raised his hand in triumph.

Suddenly, Coach Frank's voice cut through the celebration. "Get up, they're tagging up!" The two runners were trying to advance. Jesse scrambled to his feet and flung the ball—way too high—toward second, just as Coach Frank yelled "Hold it!"

The ball sailed over the shortstop and bounded into the left field corner, and the game turned into chaos. The runner going to third rushed home, and the runner sliding into second hopped up and headed for third. Salem players were shouting and pointing and jumping up and down, but no one was going to the right spots. They all just watched the third baseman and left fielder run after the ball. The second runner hit third and Coach V windmilled his arms, sending him home. The throw from the left fielder came in, looping and off-line, and the catcher ran down the first base line to grab it as the runner crossed the plate and the Peabody team went crazy. Kenny turned his back to the field. "Fuck," he bellowed.

"Double-Fuck," said KJ, who had sat up to watch. He winced and lay back down.

The next batter drilled a homer to center. 6-4, Peabody.

"Triple-fuck," said Giancarlo.

Julian doubled to lead off the 6th, but Cameron, batting in Kenny's spot—oh, how he wanted to bat!—struck out, and the next two batters did, too, ending the game with a whimper. The Peabody team mobbed each other on the mound after the last strike. The Salem players trudged up to the plate and stood waiting for Peabody to untangle themselves and line up for the postgame handshake. Kenny was the last Salem kid, sandwiched between a hunched-over KJ and all the coaches. "A couple bad breaks," Coach Cal was saying to Coach Frank.

"Line up, guys!" barked Coach V, and the Peabody boys all jogged to their side of the plate. The two teams moved forward, slapping hands. "Good game. Good game," all the Peabody kids said. The Salem kids were mostly silent. In front of Kenny, KJ limped through the line. They'd gone through all the Peabody players, and now the Peabody coaches were slapping hands. "Great game, boys!"

"Great game," Coach V said to KJ, "hope you feel better." KJ just nodded.

Coach V moved on to Kenny and put a hand on his shoulder. "Helluva game, Kenny. That slider was nasty."

Kenny tried to say, "Thanks, Coach," or "Good luck at States," but all he could get out was a grunt and a nod.

It was all so unfair.

The line ended. Kenny stood at home plate. KJ was hobbling to the dugout behind the rest of the team. He looked like a wounded bird, scrawny. Coach V and Coach Frank were talking about what a great game it had been. The Peabody players took off for a victory lap along the outfield fence, slapping hands with their fans.

Coach V, still talking with Coach Frank, turned to Kenny. "And I knew this guy was trouble," he said, grinning. His teeth seemed unnaturally white. "He plays for my AAU team. Did you know that?"

Frank nodded, "I think I did."

Kenny thought of the Angels. There was no way he was playing on that team next year, no matter what his dad said, no matter how much he had learned this year. He was done with Coach V and the legend of Peabody, their professional approach to the game. It was all bullshit. They were all bullshit. Kenny wasn't going to play on the fucking Angels next year.

But he knew he would.

No Crying

Who designed these benches? Wooden slats that imprint your back, the rest of you slipping through. It's like they wanted to remind you that you're uncomfortable, that there's as much emptiness as wood, that if one slat breaks everything becomes more dangerous. And this is a bench, something that's supposed to be a place to rest, to watch, a serene spot above the field.

Out on the diamond, the chunky boy for the White Sox, the kid who plays catcher, lines a single over the shortstop's head. He rounds first and watches the ball come back to the infield, then turns back to the base and stomps on it, satisfied. He should be. That was a nice hit. Hard. It must have felt good.

People who haven't played don't understand the feeling of hitting a ball solid. They think the ball comes in so fast it must sting the hands if you whack it, that it must take strength to turn the ball around, send it back faster than it came, and yes, if you don't hit a ball square, especially in cold weather, your hands can feel like they've been electrocuted, but hit it solid, square? When you get the ball on the bat's sweet spot? It's magical. Your body follows through so easily, the bat finishes the swing itself. It doesn't even feel physical, just a rightness, like watching the sun rise, or the way a few notes, strung together in the right rhythm, make you want to cry. It just is.

The next batter, a little waif probably a third the size of the catcher, fouls two balls off weakly, then strikes out looking. He jogs back to the dugout. He's so small. He'll probably always be small. Unfair. To go through life sensing that everyone else is bigger than you, that you're disadvantaged. To always be looking up. Then again, he could be a great jockey.

A passed ball to the next batter, and the boy on first lumbers down to second. Such is the nature of mistakes. You mess up, others take advantage. It's a simple lesson, but one that's also simple to forget.

What am I doing on this bench? Waiting for Callie. Who used to be Calvin. Who used to be my brother. Who is my sister. Who told me long ago, in the dark of our shared bedroom, that she was a girl: "I feel like a girl. Do you ever feel that way?" she said.

"No," I'd said. I was fifteen. He was thirteen. I didn't understand. It was 2004, the year that Massachusetts was debating gay marriage. In my health class, the one class where we actually talked about things, I agreed with the girls who argued for marriage equality, but I kept quiet. That night I thought that Calvin, maybe, was gay, and I felt sorry for him. And, maybe, a little sorry for myself.

The batter, a lanky kid with an inside-out swing, grounds to first, and the team in the field jogs into their dugout, like bees angling into their hive, or water descending to a drain, and the team that had been at bat fans across the field in a pattern that almost seems organized, a lovely conic outline, and the warm-up balls start flying lazily between the players. Someone who isn't in the game stands on the right field line, warming up the right fielder, while the center fielder and left fielder toss together. Does that kid like doing this? I can see now that it's the little guy, the one who struck out. Of course he is on the bench for half the game, and of course he is a kid who would help his teammates warm up. He just wants to be part of the team. He can catch the ball fine, though he always looks surprised to discover it in his glove. Oh, joy. You come in such small packages, but you're no less real for that.

Why meet here? Back in . . . it was 2001, Calvin and I were on the same team, the Cardinals. He was a ten-year-old in his first season in the majors. I was in my last. Coach Frank was our coach. Most of the players disliked Coach Frank. He'd pick on kids; "My sister throws harder than that!" he'd shout for the whole park to hear. I still remember his voice: "Justin! What are you swinging at? That pitch was over your friggin' head." Frank was a good coach, though. That's what we were told, anyway. He made us practice things that none of the other teams practiced—pick-off plays and trick steals. He had numbers for different plays—15 or 21 or 23. I still remember 23 because it meant the catcher would try to pick off the guy at first, and I was the first baseman, so I'd sneak behind the runner after the pitch. We must have tried the play twenty times that year. A couple times the throw went into the outfield. Once—just once—the play actually worked. Small joys.

Calvin was a tough little ten-year-old, one of the better ones in the league. He didn't get a lot of hits, but something in him refused to strike out, and he wouldn't swing at bad pitches. He'd stand up at the plate, a stocky righty, and only swing at the good ones. Usually, he'd swing a little late—it's hard for ten-year-olds to hit the twelve-year-olds—and he'd foul it off. I remember sometimes seeing him wince after the ball glanced the bat. Those could sting. But he'd get right back in there for the next pitch. That year he must have walked more than anyone on the team. Patient, determined. And then in the playoff game against the Cubs he got a big hit that put us ahead for good, a bouncer up the middle. I wonder if he—she—remembers that. I sure do. Calvin stoic on first base as our team went wild in the dugout, rattling the fence and screaming his name. I loved it that he didn't smile.

Three up, three down. That White Sox pitcher is good, overpowering. And that was probably the bottom of the order for the Indians. Quick inning. The strong against the weak. The twelve-year-old pitcher against the ten-year-old batters. All part of the game. One inning until it's over says the scoreboard. The White Sox ahead by three. They can smell the win. They jog into their dugout. How can I tell they're happy? I can tell they're happy.

All those years ago, we'd lost to the Indians in the City Series. Those uniforms can't be the same ones, but they look the same, with that stupid grinning red Indian on a navy background, a single feather sticking out from its headband. Racist. Yes, I learned something in my history classes. That face seemed to be laughing at us after we lost. It's hard to forget it; I saw it so much during those charged, dramatic games, the bleachers crowded with parents, the park full of curious kids whose teams hadn't made it that far. After every play there was cheering, like what we were doing meant something.

That Series was painfully close. Our best pitcher, Randy, broke his arm the day before the last game, and their third baseman made some unbelievable plays—I want to say lucky. After we had lost, Frank gathered us all around the big tree beyond the right field fence. Some of us were crying, including me. I remember that Callie—Calvin—wasn't. "I know this was disappointing, but there's no crying in baseball," Frank said as we wiped away tears and kept our heads to the ground. "You can give me your uniforms now, or on Family Day."

Callie has been Callie for almost a year now. We shared a bedroom, with bunk beds, for years, until I went off to Framingham State. When I'd come back summers, he'd be off with a few friends, down at the little beach on the other side of this park, the one that looked across the harbor to Marblehead. You can't see it from the field. You can't really even see the ocean, though it's only a couple hundred yards away. Calvin had made new friends at the high school, people who worked backstage crew for the school plays, misfits.

Baseball was long forgotten. Once he met that group, Calvin and I rarely even played PS3's Major League Baseball game anymore, something we'd been doing on rainy afternoons since elementary school. He'd try to get me to play the games he'd gotten into—Marvel: Ultimate Alliance or Gengi: Days of the Blade—and I'd play some, just to hang out with him. To be honest, they seemed like too much of a commitment, and I was busy with all those senior year parties and looking to get away, to go off to college.

I'd forgotten baseball, too. At Framingham, I studied history education, which is part history, part filling up classrooms for education professors. I've got another one-year gig at Salem High this fall. With budget cuts, it's hard to imagine it becoming permanent, but it's good for now.

One weekend when I was home from college, I went to see the high school play, and Calvin texted me from backstage, asking for a ride home. When he got into the car, his lips shone bright red. "You're wearing lipstick!" I'd said.

"Oh shit! Do you have any Vaseline?" I just looked at him. I couldn't help it. "Never mind," he said. He opened the car door. "Give me a minute." He ran back into the school and when he returned, his lips were clean.

"What was that?" I asked.

"I—" he went silent, and the look on his face made me stay silent. I started the car. A few seconds later he said, "I just like to wear it sometimes." For a moment, it was only us two and the breathing of the car's heater. The whole city disappeared.

"Oh yeah, me too," I said. I wish I hadn't joked about it like that. I was trying to let him know that I was cool with whatever, but I wish I'd said something else. I wish he'd known he could've talked to me.

The bench sags. "Hey, Justin."

It's Coach Frank, in his shiny red Cardinals windbreaker. I haven't seen him for years, but he looks the same, hefty and squat, sandy-haired, his face ruddy and impassive. When he wasn't fuming he was impassive.

"Hey, Coach." I notice the Cardinal players hanging over the outfield fence. They must have the day's second game. "Nice weather for a game. You gonna win?"

Frank shrugs. "Who knows? We got a young team."

"The Cardinals are always good," I say. I mean it. I talk to the kids at the high school. The boys remember the Cardinals. Like me, they remember Frank. The Cardinals still win a lot.

"We're alright," says Frank.

A pop-up. The first baseman calls for it, loud, just like he's supposed to, and puts it away.

I should get up, meet Callie in the parking lot. No sense having her see Frank. No sense having him see her. She never liked him. I never liked him. She's got enough going on today, leaving for Austin. "Why Austin?" I'd asked.

"Someplace new. Good music."

"But it's Texas." I'd said.

"It's not Texas. It's Austin."

Another pop-up. A weak one, and the third baseman takes two steps into foul territory and catches it easily. The batter, who didn't leave the box, pounds his bat on the ground. He must be a hitter, someone who knows he could have done better. Sometimes that confidence can carry you as a player, believing in yourself. Sometimes it can just make failure more painful.

"What are you doing down here?" Frank asks, "You know someone who's playing?"

"I'm meeting my sister." How easily I say the word "sister." It's been less than a year since she told me, but once she started wearing skirts and make-up, it wasn't hard—or as hard as I thought it would be.

"Your sister? I didn't know you had a sister."

"I do. She's moving today, to Texas. She wanted to come by here for old times' sake." Callie had texted me half an hour ago. Her car was packed. She was stopping at Hobbes to bring a few bags of popcorn to the park—what's more Salem than Hobbes popcorn? We were going to go sit on the beach, her high school haunt, before she hit the road.

"Hey, Justin," and standing there, just the other side of Frank, is Callie. She's in a lime green dress that stops just above her knees, a bag of popcorn in each hand. Her legs, of course, are shaved. Her hair is straight and comes to her shoulders. She's stocky, like he—she's?—always been, but the dress makes her seem more curvy. She started the estrogen five months ago, and she told me that she's noticing changes. To me, she looks a lot like Calvin in makeup, a girl's hairstyle, and a dress, but what do I know? I knew Calvin for a long time. I wonder what Frank sees.

"Calvin?" says Frank. The corner of his mouth jerks.

"Callie," says Callie. "Hi, Coach."

Frank's eyes take in Callie more fully. I can see that she feels him appraising her. "It's a new look," she says, and gives a quick smile—at Frank? at me?

Beyond us, there is applause. The inning has ended. The Indians come jogging in for their last at-bat.

Two Cardinals run up to Frank. One's grey pants are snug around his legs, outlining them, the other's are baggy, sagging to the ankles. Their red caps and red shirts, and the way they flitted over, make them seem a bit like cardinals. "Coach," one says, "who's pitching today?"

"Not you," says Frank. He gives a little smile.

"Who?"

"I'll tell you when I tell you. Don't ask again."

The two stand there for a second. One notices Callie and studies her as if trying to solve a math problem in his head.

"Jonelle, tuck your shirt in," Frank says to the kid.

Jonelle breaks his gaze and tucks his shirt in, then they both dash back to their teammates.

Frank leans forward on the bench. His eyes stay on the field, watching the White Sox pitcher fire his warmups. "Justin says you're moving to Texas."

"Austin," says Callie. She's looking out at the field, too. They're not looking at each other, but it's not avoidance. It's something about rituals, about what we've been taught—why we follow the speeding ball from fingers to bat to glove, why we note that the first baseman's too close to the line, the left fielder is chewing on his glove, unready. The ocean, in all its sunlit splendor, roils just beyond the leaf-heavy trees, but we're here, watching children in uniforms trying to do what they're supposed to do.

"You driving?" Frank asks.

"My car's packed. Right over there." Callie gestures beyond the outfield fence.

Frank looks over. "Texas is a long ways from here."

Callie walks in front of him, across his line of vision, to my side of the bench. I see Frank follow the swing of her dress, her sandaled feet. She hands me a bag of popcorn. On the field, the Indian batter hits a high fly, and the few fans "ooh" at its arc. It doesn't clear the fence, but the leftfielder misjudges it, and it lands behind him. There's the frenzy of action, and then the Indian batter is standing on second base, straightening his helmet with both hands. I feel happy for him, even though he's on the Indians.

"We should've beat the Indians that year," I say.

"That was a tough one," Frank says.

"If Randy hadn't gotten hurt . . .," I say.

"Yeah, and then their third baseman makes those two diving catches. The little shit hadn't caught a ball the whole season." Frank shakes his head.

"I know, I know . . .," and that last catch replays itself in my mind. Everything seemed wrong about it, like it should never have happened. The kid tripped over his feet, but that just made him dive toward the ball. And were his eyes closed? And now I see Calvin after the game ended, standing in front of me as we're in line, a head shorter than I was, slapping the Indians' hands. "Congratulations," he kept repeating in his ten-year-old voice. And suddenly I'm biting my lip, trying not to tear up.

Callie laughs. It's a laugh that's new for her, one slightly higher pitched, and one that feels, somehow, honest. Frank can't help but look at her. I can't either. She taps my shoulder. It's time to walk to the beach. Callie shakes her head, swishing her hair.

"You two," she says, smiling, "You know there's no crying. Not in baseball."

Frank and I look at each other. I was about to cry, and now, suddenly, I can't help but grin. "She's right, you know," I say, standing.

Frank strokes his chin. Was that a smile? "You know," he says, turning back to look my sister in the face, "you always had a better eye than your brother."

Prospect

Miguel dropped a dime into the slot, and mariachi music rumbled hollow from the aged machine, more noise amid the beeps and blurps and canned sounds of the arcade. And then the monkeys began moving inside the case, bouncing and nodding their heads up and down. They were seated in two rows, each about six inches high, wearing sombreros and wielding their trumpets and trombones and saxes. In the front row center, a drummer pounded his drums in a frenzy, his head flying back and forth as if it would detach from his body.

How old were they, Miguel wondered. No doubt older than he was. Their fur was patchy, worn away completely in spots, and there was something freaky about the holes that appeared in the necks whenever the heads bounced up, as if they were being decapitated. You could glimpse inside their bodies, a dark grin that opened up again and again.

When his Aunt Sarah used to bring him to the Salem Willows boardwalk as a child, these holes disturbed him, and even though his young cousin, Ricky, loved the monkeys and insisted on watching them play and dance, Miguel would find an excuse to be somewhere else. He'd wander off and watch teens playing Grand Theft Auto or air hockey, or make his way to the mini-batting cage and study boys with plenty of quarters and weak swings. Back then, the band of monkeys made him feel that Salem was old, and dusty, and haunted.

"Why'd you want to watch this?" Carmen asked. "This your kind of music?"

Miguel shrugged. "Back in Salem, man. This is what you do in Salem. Watch the monkeys."

After four years in the Dominican, Miguel had returned two months ago and had started the school year at Salem High three weeks earlier. He'd just turned 18, but since he'd missed those years, he was only a junior. Carmen was in his English class, and she went to the same church as Sarah and Miguel. When Miguel had mentioned his birthday to her in class, she'd proposed this visit to the Willows. "We should do something," she said.

The monkeys were all bouncing at their own pace, to their own rhythm. There was no way they could be playing the same song, but they had a crazy energy. "My aunt used to always play this for Ricky."

"My parents did that, too. I loved them when I was a kid," Carmen said.

Miguel was going to tell her about the necks and how he used to dislike them, but the music stopped and she grabbed his arm.

"Ice cream," she said.

They stepped out of the arcade's shade, into the afternoon light.

It was Saturday. In the grassy park between the boardwalk and the water, some families were grilling. The kids, and a few of the men, tossed and kicked balls. Their voices were a mix of Spanish and English.

The chill of early autumn had scoured the humidity from the city. Miguel thought how far a ball would travel in the dry air and wished he were on a diamond somewhere. The feeling was so strong he stopped walking and smacked his right hand into his left palm, as if he was pounding a glove.

Carmen was looking at him. "What's the matter?" she asked.

"Nothing . . . nothing."

"Then let's get some ice cream."

The breeze ruffled Carmen's short sleeves.

"It's too cold," said Miguel. "Let's get popcorn. I haven't had Hobbes in forever."

Hobbes, the place down at the end of the boardwalk, was probably older than the monkeys. Jeff Shea, Miguel's coach back in Little League, had taken the team there a few times. He'd talk about how he used to run the taffy machine back when he was a teenager. Hobbes had the best popcorn. Miguel especially liked the wintergreen, with its pink coating and fresh, bright sweetness.

They walked past the dinky storefronts: the chop suey place, the grimy pizza joint. They passed the mini-golf squeezed between two buildings, the other arcades with the empty kiddie rides that went in slow circles—cars, trains, and, out in front, boats asleep in a leaf-littered pool.

He and Carmen walked up to the counter. "Can I help you?" Miguel looked up. It was Keith Shea, Jeff's son and his old teammate on the White Sox. They had both pitched for that team, taken the Sox all the way to the city championship game. Miguel still remembered that loss, how their left-fielder dropped an easy flyball.

"Yo dude, what's up," Miguel said.

"Masher!" said Keith. Everyone on that team had called Miguel "Masher." Miguel the Masher. The two clasped hands over the counter and pulled themselves towards each other, patting each other's back and bumping chests. Keith had gotten heavy, and his face was puffy, jowly. His loose-fitting t-shirt ballooned around him almost like a dress. It was speckled with flecks of popcorn. That's Salem, Miguel thought, you work the same job your dad used to have. He wondered if Jeff was even playing ball anymore. He'd been a damn good pitcher.

"That really you? You on vay-cay from the DR?" said Keith.

"Nah, man, I'm back for good."

"For real?"

"Yeah, the DR was a trip, but it got old."

"No MLB? I was pulling for you."

"Never say never," said Miguel, but, he thought, you could probably say never. He thought of the conversation with Rafael a few months after he'd had wrist surgery. Rafael's face was flat, none of the energy he had out on the field, urging them to push harder during the sprints. It wasn't animated, like when he'd put his arm around Miguel four years earlier, the day Miguel and his uncle showed up at the compound and his uncle said, "Sí, lo está hacienda."

That day in his office, Rafael asked him about his aunt in Salem. Miguel understood. After four long years, he was no longer a prospect. Maybe, Rafael said, Miguel could go back, finish high school in the states. "Maybe play in college," he said. "You meet with the tutors, right?" Miguel nodded, though he hadn't met with the tutors much in the last year. Most evenings, local teachers came to the compound and offered lessons to the boys who wanted them, or whose families insisted upon them. Even though they felt way too simple, Miguel had liked the classes. He got to speak some English, and it was satisfying to get a math problem right. He liked it when the teachers used the kids' contracts to study percentages. Miguel's uncle, who signed the contract for him, had made sure Rafael's camp would get only 30 percent of any contract he signed with a pro team. Even if he signed for just 150 thousand, he'd get over 100 thousand. When he was thirteen, most of the kids weren't as big as he was. The Dominican was a poor country, and they hadn't ever eaten good food or enough food. A lot of these kids would have to give 40% of any signing to the compound to pay for the "nutrition supplements" they were given to bulk up their bodies.

Miguel thought of the group of kids who circled around the trainer after practice to take their daily pill. In the lessons, Miguel had teased them about how much more money he'd be getting when he signed until Luis threatened to knife him if he didn't shut up.

"Yo, let's hang sometime," said Keith. "I'm at the Tech. What's your number?"

Miguel had been asking his aunt to set him up with a phone, but he wouldn't get it until the next weekend. "Haven't got one yet. I'll find you, though." They nodded at each other.

"Can, uh, we get a bag of wintergreen?" Miguel asked.

"And a regular," added Carmen.

Keith looked at her with a slow smile. "One regular and one wintergreen."

They took their bags and walked past parents trailing toddlers. Pigeons, with a sprinkling of gulls, clustered around the garbage cans. Others strutted along the path poking at specks on the pavement. Miguel and Carmen found a bench overlooking the docks and harbor. He could see an island out beyond the harbor's mouth. He'd known the name of it once. He'd heard that a few people lived there in houses without running water or electricity. He thought about Enrique, one of the kids at the compound who, the first few weeks, kept flicking the light switches. Enrique's family, he'd heard, didn't have electricity in their house. Funny how it was the same, but not at all the same. Those people on that island had money; they used generators and hauled water out on boats. Miguel imagined the sound of the generators kicking in on a cold morning. Was it like the sound of the heat coming on in his aunt's apartment? It would be cool to see how it all worked, Miguel thought. He wondered about going out there. How would he do it?

"Were you going to play in the pros?" Carmen asked, reaching into his wintergreen bag. She pulled out a handful. Miguel gave her a cutting look. She plucked one piece from her hand and returned it to his bag, and they both laughed.

"Uh . . . yeah . . . well, I was trying to. That was the plan. It's why I was in the DR. I was at this compound in Santiago where they train players."

"For the last four years?"

"Yeah. I know. Six days a week. Off for Christmas. Two weeks in the summer."

"What did you do?"

Miguel smiled at her. "Played baseball. Day after day. Well, actually, we did drills five days a week. Scrimmaged on Saturdays. They wanted to get us ready for workouts with the major leagues."

Miguel set his bag of popcorn on the bench between them. He slid his hand under his t-shirt and ran it up his stomach to his chest. He could feel his pec, hard and broad, stretching under his palm. He felt the slow thump of his heart.

"Did you like it?" Carmen turned her gaze from the ocean to him. Was she wearing make-up? Just a little lipstick, maybe. Her hair was pulled back in a bun, nothing fancy. He liked that. "Did you?" He looked away, at the little beach nearby. It was empty. He rubbed his hand across his chest. Did he like it? There was too much to say.

"It was hot. It was hard. Some of it was fun." He turned back to her. A strand of hair blew across her face. He shrugged. "I love baseball," he said.

Carmen nodded. She seemed like she wanted to say more, but she didn't. She reached down and picked up the wintergreen bag. "You want any more?" she asked.

"I'm good," said Miguel. He removed his arm from under his shirt and rested it along the top of the bench, behind Carmen. She pulled some popcorn from the bag and leaned into him.

*

He'd flown down to the Dominican three times, though he barely remembered the first trip. He'd been three, and his mother had taken him. She had wanted to be with her family at the end of her life. Miguel just remembered running around a yard with pink flowers, a wasp stinging his thigh, and his mother's face toward the end, gaunt, with droopy eyelids, how it looked nothing like the cheery photos of her that Aunt Sarah kept in the Salem apartment.

He went back again with Sarah when he was eight and spent the whole summer with his uncle's family in Cerra Alta in north Santiago, playing baseball nonstop with his cousins, swimming off the heat in early afternoon.

And then he'd gone back there, supposedly for two weeks, when he was thirteen, and his uncle had introduced him to Rafael, who had played in the minors for the Tigers, got as far as triple A, and who helped run the local compound. Rafael liked Miguel's size and strength. "A big boy," he kept saying.

"Are you playing AAU?" Rafael had asked him. Miguel shook his head. One or two of the richer kids in Salem had played AAU, and Miguel had wanted to sign up, but he'd looked at the website on the computer in the middle school library. AAU cost 1600 dollars.

It had all happened so quickly. His uncle had the idea, and even though Sarah was against it, she told Miguel it was up to him. Some of the boys Miguel had played ball with in the Dominican had gone into Rafael's camp. Miguel was better than most of them. Maybe Miguel should go into the camp, too.

"Quieres ser un profesional, ¿verdad?" his uncle said.

"Sí."

"Nadie te va mirar allí arriba. El entrenamiento, no vas a obtener pero aquí . . . mira Gabriel."

Gabriel was a second cousin, a great baseball player. He'd gone to Rafael's camp for three years, and on signing day—July 2nd—the year he turned 16, he got a contract with the Devil Rays for 150,000 dollars. Now, Gabriel trained in the team's complex in Baseball City. He was going to play in the minors next year, Montgomery, Alabama.

Faced with the choice, Miguel had thought about Salem. Why should he go back? Sarah worked in Boston, two different jobs; it seemed like she was always either at work or on the bus. Even though he lived with her, he only saw her once or twice a week. He saw Ricky more. Ricky was eight. He and Miguel shared a room, and they ate breakfast together most mornings before Miguel shooed him out the door to catch his bus. He loved Ricky. He loved his Aunt. When they would go to church, Miguel felt like they were one more little family among all those Spanish-speaking families. I'm American, but I'm Dominican, too, Miguel used to tell his friends. Miguel's friends? Middle school would have been more fun if he had a phone, but Sarah wasn't going to buy him a phone. "Maybe in high school," she'd said.

If he stayed in the DR, he might get drafted. He might, when he was 16, get a 150-thousand-dollar contract. Or even better. Someone from

Rafael's compound had got 450 thousand from the Rangers. Even after Rafael and the other buscones took their cut, that was some serious cash. And, he'd get to play ball all year long.

At first, he'd loved it. It was so different from Salem. All the kids were players, and the practices made him feel like a professional. They would hustle on and off the field, and the ball would zip from glove to glove when they did infield. A few of the fourteen-year-olds were already hitting the ball out. He'd gotten close himself a few times.

Just like in Salem, he was bigger than the other boys his age. Some were taller, stringy boys with arms longer than baseball bats who threw harder than he could, snapping their arms like there were no joints in them, but Miguel's chest was broader than any of theirs. Luis, the whippet infielder half his size who, somehow, threw just as hard as he did, started calling him "El Toro," and the name stuck.

Even the running felt good. Sprints, and more sprints. And weights. Miguel could feel his body getting leaner and stronger; he reached a point where he could do pushups for, it seemed, forever. Soon, his pecs were like a man's, his own arms hard and thick as pipe. Lying down at night, even though he would be tired, his body felt like it was entirely muscle. He was a fist.

The compound's cinder block dorms felt empty, but crowded, too. There were three of them to a room, all sleeping on mattresses thrown on the floor. Almost none of them brought anything more than a shoebox of personal belongings. Most walls were empty, though a few had posters of major league Dominicans. The ten-foot fence around the compound kept out distractions. When he'd take balls in the outfield, sometimes he'd hear voices of children, laughing, fighting.

He learned, too late, not to trust anyone. His batting gloves were stolen twice, and, after 1000 pesos of his disappeared, he started taking any money out onto the field with him, keeping it in a baggie in the back pocket of his baseball pants.

Four years. And now he was back in Salem, back in the room he had shared with Ricky in Sarah's apartment, sharing it again. He'd gone into Salem

High with Sarah when the school year started, and the counselor was able to fudge some things and have him start as a junior. He just had to pass the MCAS at the end of the year. "So you only lose a year," she said.

"Awesome," said Miguel.

"Gracias," said his aunt.

Sometimes Miguel felt like he'd lost all four years. He'd think of day after day in the sun, the boy who would always faint and who left after the first year. He'd think of how he had gone from being one of the biggest, strongest guys to just another stocky sixteen-year-old, not one of those speedy ones who always went first in the drills, the ones who would disappear and the kids would say, "Marlins," or "Pirates," or "300,000."

He thought about the line of borax along the bathroom walls to hold off the roaches, the bologna and mayonnaise that he grew sick of, the one coach, Dario, who kept making him change his stance.

After the first two years, the scouts who would come by rarely singled him out, called him over to ask questions. Baseball was still fun, but it had come to seem like it wasn't enough, and Miguel looked forward to the two weeks off in the summer after the interbarrio tournament when he could fly back north and see his aunt and Ricky, when he'd hunt up old friends and speak English. And during the year he looked forward to Sundays, when he could get away to his uncle's house. There had been some sweet girls in Cerra Alta. A few times he and his cousins drove to the beach with them. Miguel carried in his mind one dusk behind the dunes and the way Marisol felt, her breasts, his hands pulling her ass toward him, then his fingers in her, her hand around him, the scent in the air, and, later, on his fingers.

The drive back to his uncle's, the car stereo playing American hits, he and Marisol cozy in the back seat, the windows down and the wind whipping around the car, making the night seem fresh and alive . . . it was like the beginning of a baseball season, the excitement of not knowing what was to come. The Dominican was poor, and hot, and dusty, but there was something about the way his cousins boasted about their fastballs, or the jolt of excitement when a scout showed up, chewing tobacco, standing in the shade, arms crossed.

What was there to dream in Salem? That he'd get a new cell phone? Go to North Shore Community College? He thought of his Aunt Sarah, how she spent her rare moments of free time watching a telenovela while texting with some friends from church.

Miguel gazed across the harbor. Carmen was half asleep, nestled in his arm. He thought of the next two years at Salem High. He liked the kids, and the baseball players all welcomed him back, almost like he'd never left. Still, when he thought of the teachers and lockers and crowds of teens hanging outside the front doors after the bell, he felt tired. He tried to stay in the present, to feel Carmen's ponytail pressing into his shoulder. This is good, he told himself. Life is good. But he knew—he knew—he was going nowhere. He'd left Salem, and now he was back where he started with nothing to show for it. His mind kept flashing back to those monkeys, bobbing madly. Those fucking monkeys.

*

"Whoa," Miguel said as he and Carmen stepped through the glass doors. The museum was airy. Three stories above them, the ceiling was curving glass panels, and so the inside had the mood of the outside: sunny, bright.

A man in a blue suit jacket approached them. "Welcome to the PEM," he said. "Can I help you?" He said the second sentence as if they might be lost and had wandered in by mistake.

"Um . . .," Miguel said. Maybe they could leave and just say they went. That's what some of the other boys in the class were going to do.

"We're supposed to see the Rodin exhibit," Carmen said, "for school."

"Our teacher made us come," said Miguel.

"Made you come?" the attendant smiled. Carmen laughed.

"Well, not made . . . it's an assignment."

"We're Salem residents," Carmen said. "We get in free, right?"

"That's right. Just go over to the desk and show some form of i.d."

Miguel was glad Ms. Sherwood had told them to bring their student i.d.s. They got little tags at the desk and followed the signs upstairs. Miguel remembered coming here once before, in third grade. His class had all written poems about paintings of boats. His, he remembered, had made his teacher laugh.

"It's so echoey," Carmen said.

"It's so echoey," said Miguel.

She laughed and pushed his arm. "Funny."

On the third floor, Miguel pulled open the door and they stepped in. It was dark—no windows, no glass ceiling—and crowded. There were a lot of people, most of them older women, dressed bright and flowery, like his abuela back in the DR, though they were white and spoke English. Miguel wondered if anyone in the room spoke Spanish. The security guard had skin darker than his. Maybe him. He'd nodded at Miguel when he and Carmen had walked in.

"We should speak English here," Miguel said.

Carmen smiled. "Sí, we should." She drew out the word "should," and Miguel wondered if she was going to be mischievous. In Ms. Sherwood's class, she was full of mischief. "Macho Man," she'd say, mocking the guys when they talked boastfully about women. She made Miguel smile. After that day at the Willows, they'd agreed to walk to church together, and then Carmen had asked Miguel to the movies, and he'd said yes before he even thought about it, and after they spent that night kissing in the theater, they'd decided to go out.

A cluster of people were standing in front of a wall and reading about Rodin. Miguel stood with them and started to read, too, but Carmen grabbed his arm. "C'mon. We're not here to read." She pulled him to a bronze sculpture of a hand. It was black and was bigger than Miguel's head. "Clenched Hand," the caption read. The fingers were all bent, kind of like it was going to throw a knuckleball.

There were other hands, too. One in a glass case read, "Hand of the Devil." Miguel fingered the cross around his neck. The hand was twice as big as a human hand, and it held a person in its palm, its fingers curving like bars around it. The Devil's hand.

In a glass case next to it was a much bigger hand, the size of a luggage: "The Hand of God." This one seemed unfinished. The hand rose out of a block of stone, and the two figures held in the palm hadn't been chiseled fully out of the marble that surrounded them. Why was one hand God's and one the Devil's? Miguel turned from one to the other. God's hand was bigger—was that it? God's hand wasn't finished; it came out of the marble, but there was still raw stone around parts of the hand and the figures in it. Was that supposed to mean that God's work wasn't finished? That was a cool idea. And God was holding two bodies that were entangled in a topsy-turvy embrace.

Miguel thought about Marisol and the beach and the sand sticking to his back after he got up. How she brushed it off and he'd felt like he was a kind of statue that was being discovered, unveiled. It was like his back could suddenly feel the light of the newly risen moon. He looked closer at the bodies curling into each other. A woman and a man, so curved they seemed like they could only hold their pose if they were underwater. They needed God to hold them together. The man had his hands on the woman's head. She was looking down at him. They were about to kiss.

Miguel looked up to find Carmen. She was studying another hand across the room, her fingers over her slightly opened mouth. He looked back at the hand of God and imagined him and Carmen in that pose. Maybe if they had a hammock, something that could hold them off the ground, that would let them float together.

Together. Miguel stepped back and looked at the Devil's hand. The body it held was all alone. Was that the difference between God and the Devil—the Devil took you when you were alone? Miguel stepped to the right and—and the body had no head! Had it broken off? Or was it supposed to be like that? Miguel thought about how the hand of God had too much marble. Here, the Devil took too much. By making a body, the devil killed it. Miguel felt his own wrist ache from where he had broken it last year. It made a kind of sense to him, and he noticed the legs of the body in the Devil's palm, how they bent sharply at the knee, and how they deteriorated down to the twisted, deformed blobs of feet. The calves had no muscle; they looked like overcooked asparagus. Miguel suddenly remembered a game way back in Little League when Ramon, one of the kids on his team, had gotten badly hurt when another kid slid into him. Ramon's leg had bent in a way that was unnatural, and he'd screamed, and an ambulance came out and they carried him away. His limp body in their locked arms looked like this body in the hand of the Devil.

Miguel thought about what it must be like to get old.

He rubbed his palm over the scar on his wrist and walked across the room to Carmen, who was reading a placard in front of a sculpture of two people entangled like the figures in God's hand. These two were standing, though. They were two feet high, and, as Miguel got closer, he saw that the man looked more like a monster, clawing the woman from behind, his face wild and hairy, one hand coming up between the woman's legs, and her hand down there, too, covering herself. The woman was leaning away from the male creature's head, lifting her shoulder in defense.

Carmen turned to him. "This is the Minotaur," she said. "Remember when we did mythology, the guy in the maze who was half-bull, half-man?"

"Oh yeah," Miguel said, "He ate people and their bones were all around."

"He looks like he's going to eat her," Carmen giggled.

"He probably is," said Miguel.

"It says he represents bestial sexuality," said Carmen.

"Kind of disturbing," said Miguel. He noticed that he was standing behind Carmen like the Minotaur was behind the woman. He moved up beside her.

"Maybe we should write about this," Carmen said.

Miguel knew he wouldn't write about this. He was fascinated by the figures all twisted together, how he could see the definition in their legs and shoulders. When he thought about the Hand of God, he felt . . . he felt like he had gotten closer to God, and now, looking at the Minotaur, its open mouth, that hand between the legs, that phrase, "bestial sexuality," he felt shame. He was not going to write about this. It would be like taking off his shirt in front of Ms. Sherwood, sitting in class topless.

Miguel leaned closer to Carmen, so his arm touched her shoulder. She tilted her head toward him. Her hair fell on his arm. It tickled. It tingled.

His right arm. The one he'd thrown thousands and thousands of balls with. He remembered the tryout with the guy from the Cubs, how he'd felt so quick, so strong, and he'd backhanded a ball, planted, and then flung the ball wide and short. He could see it bouncing then rolling to the fence, how it carried his major league dream with it into the dirt on the field's edge.

When Miguel and Carmen walked out of the museum, the saxophone player on the cobblestones, the scent of fried dough and sausages from the tourist carts, and the gusts of autumn, all cast such a spell that they almost got hit by the tourist trolley, and then Carmen couldn't stop laughing. With money from his job as a line cook, Miguel bought burritos and sodas, and they sat on a stone wall in the park next to the Visitor's Center. Suddenly Carmen stood. "Napkins," she said, and walked back across the street to the burrito place.

Miguel looked at her burrito, which she'd left on the wall, shiny in its tin foil. The silver stood out against the natural greys of the rock. It caught the sun and spread it across the day. Miguel thought of the Dominican sun, so relentlessly hot. He took a swig of his root beer, then looked at the bottle in his hand. His fingers curled around it, four on one side, opposite his thumb. When he held a baseball, only two fingers, the index and pointer, were on one side. His pinkie, ring finger, and thumb curved around the ball, holding it in place before the arm thrust forward and the hand opened in release. He put his soda down and tried to shape his hand as if it were holding a ball.

It looked like—it looked like the hand of God. Miguel turned his wrist so that his palm was face up to the sky. Now it looked like the hand of the Devil. He imagined holding a small body in his palm, rather than a baseball, and his fingers curled a little differently. He didn't want to hurt it, but he needed to support it.

"What are you doing?" asked Carmen. A bouquet of napkins spread out from her hand.

"Nothing."

"You were doing something."

Carmen was smiling at him, like she knew his secret, but he didn't know he had a secret. He knew he'd seen the hand of God, and the hand of the Devil, right here in his hometown. He knew he'd never forget that.

Some tourists were walking by, eyes hidden behind sunglasses, poking their phones, trying to find out where they were. *You're in Salem,* Miguel wanted to say, *Salem, Massachusetts. U.S.A.* One woman, head down, almost walked straight into Carmen, then stepped around her without acknowledging her. Carmen looked at Miguel and rolled her eyes. Miguel almost called out to the woman, *She lives here. I live here.*

"Well?" Carmen said.

Miguel grinned back at her and lifted his right arm in between them. He twisted his fingers, trying to recreate the shape of Rodin's sculpture, "The hand of God," he said, "I was making the hand of God."

Today, late April,

the sun out after a morning of rain, a few drying puddles, some damp dead leaves, winter's leftovers, in the gutters, scattered twigs like arthritic worms on the sidewalks, the leavings of last night's wind, and I'm walking the two blocks from the college to the park, past the houses of my sons' childhood friends, past the rented houses crammed with students, downhill to the park's entrance, the Little League field fluorescent green in the sun-soaked afternoon, the Atlantic barely visible down the drive that follows the outfield fence and curves into the rest of the park, chips of white flashing in its slate, and I step past the untended gatehouse where some teen in a bright t-shirt will check cars for resident stickers once summer spreads itself across the year and the outdoor pool opens in the park's far corner, and out in front of me, on the diamond, a tall Latino man in a bright red t-shirt and red cap pitches to his son, his other son chasing the balls down in the outfield, and as I watch the son running through the outfield toward the chain-link fence, the wave of all those years spent with my two sons on baseball diamonds breaks through me, nearly toppling me, a weight not of memories—no swirling collage of moments—but feeling, ineffable and thick as the muddy batters' box that only here, setting the moment down in words, am I able to fasten to actual bits of past: how there would be afternoons when I would get lost wondering whether my son would hit a ball hard that evening, how there would be days when I'd hit groundball, groundball, groundball to my eldest while my youngest, worn out or bored, would climb a tree and read a book, how my arm would hurl pitches until it hung, exhausted, some instrument that was less a part of my body than a marvelous aged machine whose workings I would never understand, and if the world was timeless, like a poem, I would have sat on the small, unbalanced, aluminum bleachers and watched the father and sons, studying the boys' swings, assessing the father's accuracy, breeze billowing my unzipped windbreaker as I let all that once was have a second, shaky life in my cells; a ball might have even, in a moment of triumph for the boy, and the father, cleared the fence—a home run! even though it was only practice—and I'd jump from my seat, a twinge in the knees, and jog to it, slow to a walk as I approached it lying there in the rut made by some long-gone car, a dirt-stained ball beside glistening grass, and bend, the ball fitting my hand with the beautiful solidity of a fact, and I brush off a nub of mud and turn toward the field—they are all looking at me—and cock my arm and flick the ball back over the fence to the glove of the brother, a boy whose name I will never know.

1625

Those who lived here called it
what they called themselves, "Naumkeag,"
the fishing place. The fish were huge back then,
though, back then, that was just what fish were.

Almost no one spoke English.
There were no petitions
to stop the persecution,
no ammunition bunkers on Winter Island.

The immigrants hadn't yet chosen here,
but they would, and, in time,
the wharves emerged, splayed fingers
clutching the sea and its bounty.
And then a nation's first millionaire,
first telephone. The founder of kindergarten.

In 1625, there was no secret staircase,
no gables, no toxins in the soil
on the banks of North River.
No cellphones, no drones.

Looking backward, we can see what wasn't,
and then what was. Cautions and wonders.

In this city unafraid of the undead,
the popcorn at the Willows is still
the best around, and the new pier
is a good place to fish.

Notes

Salem Common on Training Day, 1808: This painting can be found at the Peabody Essex Museum in Salem.

"Two Voices from the Trials": Incorporates some of Mary Towne Eastey's second petition to the governor.

The map of the Salem Fire, *Conflagration-Salem, Mass.*, is published courtesy of Nelson Dionne Salem History Collection, Salem State University Archives and Special Collections, Salem, Massachusetts.

"What Is": Nancy Harrington, Salem State's first woman president, passed away in 2020. Salem State's central campus was renamed "Harrington Campus" in a ceremony in 2021.

"1625": This poem was written and read for Salem's "State of the City" event, January 2025.

Acknowledgments

Thanks to the editors and publishers of the magazines and books where the following first appeared:

"Salem, Mass," *Drunk Monkeys*, *Lifting the Turtle*

"Prayer," *Lifting the Turtle* (under the title "Prayer to My People")

"Montage of Brick and Water," *Salem: Place, Myth and Memory*, *The Last Miles* (a different version of the single poem "Yellow Leaves on a Blue Plastic Slide" originally appeared in *Lifting the Turtle*)

"High Street Park: The Kindness of Boys," *Pangyrus*

"No Heaven," *The Quotable*

"Salem Common," *Ekphrastic Review*, *Lifting the Turtle*

"Two Voices from the Trials" are excerpted from the script *Imprisoned! 1692* co-written with Cindy Veach and produced by Essex National Heritage Area.

"The Great Fire," *Solstice*

"Laid-Off Elementary School Librarian," *Drunk Monkeys*, *Lifting the Turtle*

"Winter Island Vow," *Lifting the Turtle* (as "The Vow")

"Breathing," *The Chronicle of Higher Education*, *Themes for English B: A Professor's Education In and Out of Class*

"A Good School," *Boston Globe Magazine*, *Themes for English B: A Professor's Education In and Out of Class*

"It Grows Back: Three Students," *Solstice*

"The Swans of Charter Street," *Themes for English B: A Professor's Education In and Out of Class*

"Racist," *The Lowell Review*

"No Crying," *Solstice*

"Today, late April," *Sport Literate*

Poems from *Lifting the Turtle* used with permission, WordTech Communications LLC, Cincinnati, Ohio, (C) 2017.

Essays from *Themes for English B: A Professor's Education In and Out of Class* used with permission, University of Georgia Press.

*

Many thanks to Paul Marion, Rosemary Noon and Loom Press for their belief in this work and editorial advice.

Thanks also to Salem State University and the Salem Athenæum, two institutions that sustained me and became like home for me.

A writing residency at the T.S. Eliot House in Gloucester, Massachusetts, provided support to complete this book.

Thanks to Brooke Delp for her sharp eyes.

And thanks to those who supported me, in various ways, as I wrote my way through Salem:

Kathleen Aguero, Benji Aul, Suzanna Baird, Brian Brodeur, Patricia Buchanan, Patricia Ann Callan, Shari Caplan, Kevin Carey, MP Carver, Scott Chiasson, Caitlin Corbett, Beth Ann Cornell, JD Debris, Jim DeFelippi, Brooke Delp, Bryan Desjardins, P. John Eakin, Cathy Fahey, Alan Feldman, Lisa Fowler, Karen Gahagan, Alison Gerber, Jack Giour, Gregory Glenn, Charlotte Gordon, Jeffrey Harrison, Gregg Higgins, Richard Hoffman, Lis Horowitz, Jennifer Jean, Danielle Jones, Claire Keyes, Kali Lightfoot, Rod Kessler, Marc Levy, Kevin McCarthy, Michael McInnis, Carolyn Maguire, Jennifer Martelli, Colleen Michaels, Anne Noonan, Scott Nowka, Joe O'Day, January Gill O'Neil, Carla Panciera, Dawn Paul, Jean Marie Procious, Peter Sampieri, Nancy Lusignan Schultz, Mark Stevick, Phillip Swanson, Mingyue Tao, Ann Taylor, Heather Treseler, Keja Valens, Cindy Veach, C. Julie Whitlow, Heather Wright, and Clay Ventre.

Much love and thanks to all my family, including my parents, James and Christine Scrimgeour; my siblings, Xanthi and Jamie, and their families; and my Kansas City family.

To Eileen, Aidan, and Guthrie, thanks for being on this journey with me. As the sundial in the Ropes Garden says,

Hours fly

Flowers bloom and die

Old days, old ways

Pass by

Love stays

About the Author

J.D. Scrimgeour is the inaugural poet laureate of Salem, Massachusetts, and has lived in the city since 1996 with his wife, Eileen FitzGerald. He is the author of six books of poetry, the most recent being *Small, Rectangular, Reflected World* (Nixes Mate, 2025). His previous collection was the bilingual 香蕉面包 *Banana Bread*, written as a way to practice learning Mandarin during the Covid pandemic. Scrimgeour's second book of nonfiction, *Themes for English B: A Professor's Education In & Out of Class* won the Association of Writers and Writing Program's (AWP) Award for Nonfiction. Scrimgeour has also done various interdisciplinary work. With musician Philip Swanson he released *Ogunquit & Other Works,* a CD blending music and poetry, and with his two sons, Aidan and Guthrie, he wrote the musical, *Only Human*, which was performed in Salem's Ames Hall.

Scrimgeour has taught at Salem State University for 30 years, where he has served as Chair of English, Coordinator of Creative Writing, First Year Experience Faculty Fellow, and Liaison for the University's 1-2-1 dual-degree program with Nanjing Normal University in China. He has received the University's Senior Award for Faculty, the Global Achievement Award from the Center for International Education, and the Martin Luther King Jr. Leadership Award for "outstanding and significant contributions to the causes of freedom, justice, and equality."

His writing has won awards from the Academy of American Poets, Creative Nonfiction Magazine, the Massachusetts Cultural Council, the National Society of Arts & Letters, and the Salem Cultural Council, and he was named the 2023 Gregory Stockmal Memorial Reader for 2023 by the Worcester County Poetry Association. He also received the Salem Athenaeum's Edward Augustus Holyoke Award for "exemplary leadership cultivating a community of writers," and he was awarded a 2025 writing residency at the T.S. Eliot House in Gloucester, Massachusetts.